AUDIT-PROOF TAX SHELTERS

DONALD J. KORN

PRENTICE HALL
Englewood Cliffs, New Jersey 07632

Prentice-Hall International (UK) Limited, *London*
Prentice-Hall of Australia, Pty. Limited, *Sydney*
Prentice-Hall of Canada, Inc., *Toronto*
Prentice-Hall Hispanoamericana, S.A., *Mexico*
Prentice-Hall of India Private Limited, *New Delhi*
Prentice-Hall of Japan, Inc., *Tokyo*
Simon & Schuster Asia Pte. Ltd., *Singapore*
Editora Prentice-Hall do Brasil, Ltda., *Rio de Janeiro*

© 1993 *by*

Donald J. Korn

10 9 8 7 6 5 4 3 2 1

This publication is designed to provide accurate and authorative information in regard to the
subject matter covered. It is sold with the understanding that the publisher is not engaged in
rendering legal, accounting, or other professional service. If legal advice or other expert
assistance is required, the services of a competent professional person should be sought.

From a Declaration of Principles Jointly Adopted by
a Committee of the American Bar Association
and a Committee of Publishers and Associations.

Library of Congress Cataloging-in-Publication Data

Korn, Donald Jay.
    Audit-proof tax shelters / Donald J. Korn.
        p.   cm.
    Includes index.
    1. Tax shelters—Law and legislation—United States—Popular works.
    I. Title.
    KF6297.5.Z9K67   1993
    343.7305'23—dc20
    [347.303523]   93-26761
                                                                    CIP

ISBN 0-13-050931-0

PRENTICE HALL
Career and Personal Development
Englewood Cliffs, NJ 07632
Simon & Schuster, A Paramount Communications Company

PRINTED IN THE UNITED STATES OF AMERICA

Dedication

To Marilyn, Michelle, and Alex,
Who keep getting better

Table of Contents

Acknowledgments

For making this book possible, I'd like to thank Lisa Ross, for all of her patience and persistence; Joe Tessitore, for standing by me, and Drew Dreeland, for his kind words; Joel Nadel, who brought me into this world; Steve Kaufman, Sally Scanlon Monaghan, Noreen Perrotta, Phil Springer, Evan Simonoff, Jo-Ann Wasserman, Don Battle, Bob Casey, Dick Howard, Sandy Franks, Joe Tinkelman, Vita Nelson, and all the others who have kept me here.

Introduction

When "everyone" "knows" something, you can be sure the conventional wisdom comes up short.

For example, everyone knows that tax shelters are dead. They were killed by the Tax Reform Act of 1986. That was the deal—the death of tax shelters in exchange for an across-the-board lowering of income-tax rates.

Similarly, everyone knows that tax shelters, when they existed, were tools of the Devil. They were the means by which the despicable rich shirked their duty and avoided paying their "fair share" of the national tax bill. In turn, this increased the burden on less-prosperous, harder-working Americans.

Another universal verity is that real estate has been a disastrous investment since the mid-1980s, especially since the October 1987 stock-market crash crushed the financial markets. Of all real-estate investors, the worst off are those who participated through widely promoted syndicated limited partnerships, a long-winded way of saying "swindle."

Well, here's something everybody doesn't know.

The 1986 Tax Reform Act actually created a brand-new tax shelter—a special credit for building or rehabilitating housing stock for rent to low-income tenants. Since 1987, when the tax credit went into effect, hundreds of millions of dollars have been invested in low-income housing. Most of the money has been raised through syndicated limited partnerships.

Investors in these partnerships haven't been victimized. Far from it. The real estate they now own, tens of thousands of apartments, is nearly 100 percent occupied. Investors have earned 15 percent, 16 percent, even 18 percent per year in tax savings. That's like earning 25 percent on a CD and paying income tax on the interest.

What's more, these investors haven't exploited their fellow taxpayers. Again, far from it. They've provided decent, affordable housing for the elderly and the working poor or near-poor. Typically, tenants pay no more than 30 percent of their income for rent. *The New York Times* has praised these tax credits in an editorial; President Clinton has called for their renewal. Truly, here is a tax shelter everyone loves.

Not every tax shelter is an exercise in public spirit, but there are shelters in which you lend money for public works or give money to worthy charities. Other shelters provide housing, secure retirement, and protection for your own family. With all these options, you can shelter yourself from taxes and sleep at night with a clear conscience.

You also can chop your tax bill without worrying that the next day's mail will bring a dreaded IRS notice. You can if you follow the advice in this book: Don't hide income, don't take phantom deductions. Instead, use tax shelters that have been approved by Congress and are fully supported by IRS rulings and court decisions. The IRS won't come after you. Even if you are examined, the tax shelters in this book are so clear-cut you won't have to worry about being assessed for back taxes, interest, or penalties.

Most taxpayers find the Internal Revenue Code confusing and intimidating. They don't understand how to use tax credits and deductions. Constant changes in the tax code only compound the problem.

Not only are taxpayers confused, they're often afraid to try tax-cutting strategies for fear they'll incur the wrath of the IRS. Some of this confusion and fear is well founded. The tax code *is* complex and the IRS does have certain red flags it will attack relentlessly. Nevertheless, there are many simple safe harbors for taxpayers. There are tax benefits easily understood by anyone who's able to earn a living and run up a tax bill. What's more, these tax benefits are so well established in the law that the IRS has no interest in challenging them.

That's the purpose of this book: to spell out, in simple language, tax shelters available to ordinary working Americans. No tax frauds, no tax protests, no tax havens. Real tax shelters that work.

Moreover, these tax shelters are audit-proof. In the vast majority of instances, they're so accepted that the IRS won't even question them. In case of an IRS examination, these shelters will stand up without expensive negotiations or litigation.

You can cut your taxes, legally and ethically. All it takes is a little effort to find out which tax shelters still work.

Deduct Now, Retire at Ease

Making the Most of Your 401(K) Plan

1

James and Mary K. don't look like millionaires in the making. James works as a salesman for a paper company, Mary runs her own business as a communications consultant. Together, they earn about $70,000, not bad for a couple in their early thirties, but a long way from Ted Turner and Jane Fonda.

James and Mary aren't slouches, though. They plan to retire in the year 2014, when they're in their mid-fifties. By that time, they figure they'll have over $1 million, more than enough to put their kids through college and still support their golfing and skiing and mountain biking.

How will James and Mary amass a fortune from their modest incomes? By using the best tax shelter available to Americans today: qualified retirement plans. James contributes the maximum to his company's 401(k) plan while Mary does the same with her simplified employee pension (SEP) plan. By making tax-deductible contributions and enjoying tax-deferred compounding, assuming 10 percent growth (about the average long-term return for stock mutual funds), James and Mary will build a seven-figure fortune in 20 years. Moreover, they'll reap these tax breaks without worrying at all about threatening visits from the IRS.

POLITICALLY CORRECT

Of all the shelters left in the tax code, the safest, most lucrative are in the retirement-planning area. Here's why they're so safe:

- They're politically sacrosanct, far more likely to be expanded than cut back.
- They can be funded by low-risk investments, such as bank accounts, blue-chip stocks, and high-grade bonds.
- If you follow the rules, there's virtually no chance you'll be challenged by the IRS.

They're lucrative because they offer two shelters in one. For the most part, contributions are fully deductible. That is, a $1,000 contribution to a retirement plan cuts your taxable income by $1,000. Moreover, the investment income on that $1,000 won't be taxed immediately. If you earn 6 percent , for example, $1,000 will become $1,060, $1,123.60, and so on, with no taxes taken out. Those taxes are deferred until you take money out.

Tax deferral can make a huge difference. Suppose, for example, you invest $5,000 per year for 25 years, earning a steady 9 percent . If you had to pay 31 percent income tax each year, your $125,000 in contributions would grow to just over $300,000.

However, suppose you put $5,000 a year into a tax-deferred retirement plan. Paying no current tax, your $125,000 would grow to more than $460,000. Even after paying tax on distributions, you'd be way ahead with a tax-deferred plan.

MAKING THE MOST OF YOUR EMPLOYER'S RETIREMENT PLAN

Your retirement plan may be provided by your employer. The traditional "pension" plan, technically called a defined-benefit plan, is often offered by large companies and government agencies. As the name suggests, a pension plan is designed to provide you with a certain benefit (that is, income) in retirement. Typically, this benefit is a function of the years you worked for the organization and your income over the years.

For example, Mike has worked for Universal Exports for 30 years, working his way up to a $50,000 salary as a middle manager. When he retires at age 65, he's entitled to a monthly pension of $1,500 a month, for the rest of his life.

However, if he dies after two years, his pension stops. Thus, his wife, Nancy, who will not receive a pension, is vulnerable. As is commonly the case, Universal Export gives Mike the choice of a joint-and-survivor pension. They'll get less each month (perhaps $1,200), but the check will continue to come in while either spouse still lives. In fact, if Mike decides not to take the joint-and-survivor option, Nancy must sign a form, giving her approval.

With a defined-benefit plan, the employer bears all the risks. Universal Export is obligated to pay Mike the promised pension, for the rest of his life and perhaps for Nancy's lifetime as well. What's more, Universal Export must make payments into a special trust each year while Mike is working to ensure that the money will be there when Mike retires. Those payments must be made, good years or bad. For an organization with many employees, this can be a huge burden, especially in down years.

SHIFTING THE RISK

Therefore, many employers are shifting from defined-benefit plans, where they bear the risk, to a different type of retirement plan: defined-contribution plans. These are not really pension plans, because employees don't get a guaranteed retirement income. You may get more or less, depending on investment results. In essence, your employer makes a contribution to your account and...that's it. You bear the risks because your retirement income depends on how well the fund is managed, over the long-term.

(It's true that your employer has a "fiduciary responsibility" to see that the fund is managed prudently. But prudent money management might yield 3 percent, 6 percent, 10 percent, or more per year; there's a huge difference between good and mediocre money management, over a period of decades.)

You probably don't need to know all about defined-contribution plans, but they come in two basic varieties: money-purchase and profit-sharing plans. Money-purchase plans require the employer to make a certain level of contributions, while profit-sharing plans don't. For that reason, profit-sharing plans are becoming the most popular form of employer-sponsored retirement plan. In good years, the employer can make a sizable contribution, up to certain limits; in poor years, the employer can make a small contribution or even skip a contribution altogether.

Now, all this may be beyond your control as an employee. If your employer makes a contribution to your retirement account, defined-benefit, or defined-contribution plan, all well and good. The money will compound, free of income tax, until you make a withdrawal. The tax deduction for the contribution goes to your employer. There's not much you can do about it.

BIG NUMBERS IN 401(k)

However, employees increasingly play a role in their employer-sponsored retirement plans. The trend, as mentioned, has been from defined-benefit to defined-contribution plans; among defined-contribution plans, the trend has been to profit-sharing rather than money-purchase plans; in the late 1980s to early 1990s, the action among profit-sharing plans has been in 401(k) plans, which are becoming the dominant form of employee-retirement plans. During 1989–1991, 42,000 employers terminated traditional pension plans, while 401(k)s went from nowhere to over 100,000 plans.

Under a section of the Internal Revenue Code for which 401(k) plans are named, employers permit employees to defer a portion of their income. The income tax is deferred, too.

For example, Paula earns $32,000 a year. Her company sponsors a 401(k) plan. She elects to defer $3,000 worth of income. Now, she actually receives $29,000 a year, on which she'll owe income tax. The other $3,000—untaxed—is contributed to her 401(k) account.

If Paula had not made the 401(k) election, the $3,000 would have been subject to a 28 percent federal tax ($840) plus any state and local income taxes that apply. Paula would have wound up with around $2,000, not $3,000, to put into retirement savings.

With a 401(k), you can defer up to 20 percent of your income. (Many employers, though, set lower limits.) Paula doesn't think she'll have enough to live on if she takes a full 20 percent deduction—$6,400 of her $32,000 base salary—so she elects to defer only $3,000, less than 10 percent.

If you earn more than $45,000 a year, another limit may come into play—there's a maximum 401(k) deferral. In 1993, that upper limit is around $9,000. Each year, the upper limit increases to reflect inflation.

ROLL YOUR OWN

With a 401(k), you make all the important decisions. One decision is whether or not to participate; another is to pick a contribution amount, up to your company's limit.

From a tax viewpoint, the maximum deferral is best. The more you defer, the more tax you save and the more money you'll have in your account for tax-free accumulation.

You can't, however, always run your life by the tax code. Not everyone can afford a 20 percent salary reduction or a $9,000 cut in pre-tax income. You shouldn't reduce your income to the point where your lifestyle is crimped.

Frequently, your employer will "match" your 401(k) contributions. If you defer $3,000 worth of your income, your employer might kick in another $750, $1,500, $3,000, or even more to your account, in cash or company stock, which won't be taxed to you right away. (A 50-cent-per-dollar contribution is the norm.) If so, contribute as much as you can, because this is the closest thing to "free money" you'll ever receive.

At the end of 1992, *Money* magazine calculated the benefit of a 401(k) to a 25 year old earning $25,000 a year who would receive a 4 percent raise each year until age 65. That employee invests 6 percent of his salary and earns 9 percent a year. Outside the 401(k), he pays a 30 percent tax each year.

Here are the results after 40 years, at age 65:

| Outside 401(k) | $ 472,778 |
| Inside 401(k) | $ 877,296 |

Going one step further, assume a 50 percent matching contribution by the employer:

| Inside 401(k) with employer match | $1,315,944 |

This is not a true comparison because the 401(k) proceeds will be taxed as they're withdrawn. Nevertheless, the 401(k) plan will turn out to be a better performer, even after income taxes are paid. An employer match makes a good deal even better.

LOAN ARRANGERS

Before making any contributions, look hard at the provisions of your employer's 401(k) plans. Most plans permit withdrawals in certain circumstances, such as medical emergencies, college bills, or financial hardship. Rather than take withdrawals, you're better off borrowing, which many plans also allow.

Loans will be allowed only if your employer has a written document in its retirement plan, spelling out the:

- Identity of the people authorized to make loans.
- Loan-application procedure.
- Criteria for approving loan applications.
- Limitations on the types and amounts of loans offered.
- Procedure for determining a reasonable rate of interest.
- Type of collateral necessary to secure a loan.
- Events constituting default.
- Steps that will be taken in case of default.

Request and read this document before applying for a retirement-plan loan. That's the quickest way to learn the ground rules.

If you borrow, you generally can get your hands on your 401(k) money without paying a penalty. Interest on these loans usually is 1 percent or so over the prime rate, which is about as low a rate as you'll get anywhere. Besides, you're paying the interest to your own 401(k) account, not to a bank. (Unfortunately, the interest is not tax deductible.)

Loans must be repaid within five years but you may take longer if the money is used for a down payment on a house. Frequently, borrowing from your employer's 401(k) plan is a lot less painful and stressful than dealing with a bank.

If you withdraw rather than borrow, you'll owe income tax plus a 10 percent penalty tax on withdrawals before age 59-1/2. Obviously, a 401(k) plan with a loan provision is appealing because you can get your hands on your money at a lower cost.

LITTLE VENTURED, LITTLE GAINED

Don't be too conservative with your 401(k) money. Typically, 401(k) participants are offered a range of choices for their contributions. At the end of 1992, the largest segment (31 percent) of all 401(k) money was invested in guaranteed investment contracts (GICs), which pay a fixed amount for a fixed period, after which the interest rate is reset.

GICs are guaranteed, but only by the issuing insurance company, or by a pool of insurers. Some GICs have run into trouble when insurers encountered financial woes. Honeywell, just to name one company, offered GICs issued by Executive Life, to which employees contributed $70 million. State regulators seized the insurer in April 1991, the GIC assets were frozen, and Honeywell employees still had no access to that money at the time of this writing, two years later. Not surprisingly, some Honeywell employees have sued.

Moreover, returns have been low: for the five years through 1992, GICs averaged 8.7 percent a year, behind mutual funds that paid 10 percent–12 percent. When you're dealing with long-term retirement money, compounding free of income tax, an extra point or two can mean a great deal. For example, $1,000 grows to around $8,000 in 24 years at 9 percent; that same $1,000 grows to about $16,000 in 24 years at 12 percent.

The next highest allocation (30 percent) of 401(k) money is in employer's stock. That may be fine, if your employer is Wal-Mart or Coca-Cola. Most employees, though, already have enough of their lives tied to their company's fortunes. If your company hits hard times and is forced to lay off people, including yourself, you certainly don't want a lot of your 401(k) money in the company's stock. It's better to diversify.

Even if you're not worried about layoffs, you don't want too much of your retirement fund in one investment. Ford's stock, for example, tumbled heavily in 1990–1992 and its employees' 401(k) plans, heavily weighted in the stock, lost an average of 2.3 percent per year. By contrast, IBM's employees, who wisely put only 1 percent of their 401(k) money into the company's stock, gained 12.7 percent per year, on average, despite the fall in IBM's stock price.

How should you invest 401(k) money? A great deal depends on the shape of your portfolio, as explained on page 23. In brief, if you have extensive stock holdings outside your 401(k) plan, emphasize bond funds inside the plan. If the 401(k) plan represents most of your savings, hold a mix of stock and bond funds or a "balanced" fund that holds both.

Perhaps most important, contribute to your 401(k) plan if you possibly can. Nearly 30 percent of eligible employees fail to do so. They're missing out on one of the best audit-proof tax shelters around.

MUSCULAR FLEX

If you understand how 401(k) plans work, you'll appreciate the virtues of flexible spending accounts (FSAs), offered by some employers, especially for medical care and dependent care. Your employer will set an FSA limit, usually $2,000 to $5,000 per year. You decide how much of your salary you want to divert into the FSA, up to this limit.

Just as in the case of a 401(k) plan, reducing your salary reduces your income tax. A $5,000 reduction cuts your tax bill by $1,500 per year in a 30 percent bracket. Yet you can buy $5,000 worth of dependent care, for example, or medical expenses (for example, eyeglasses, dental bills) otherwise not reimbursed by health insurance. The bottom line is that you receive $5,000 worth of goods or services yet give up only $3,500 in net income, so the FSA would save you $1,500.

The tax savings are even greater if your compensation is below $55,000 or so, because reducing your income also reduces your Social Security (FICA) taxes.

The drawback? FSA money is "use it or lose it." If you put $5,000 into an FSA and use only $4,000 during the year, you won't get the extra $1,000 and it won't carry over into the next year. So be careful in how much you put into an FSA and be sure to use up all the money. Nevertheless, FSA are great tax shelters, as audit-proof as 401(k)s, and they should be used as much as practical.

SUMMING UP

- Retirement plans are prime tax shelters so they should be funded to the greatest extent possible.
- Employers are shifting from defined-benefit (pension) plans, where they bear the risk, to defined-contribution plans, where you bear the risk.
- Among defined-contribution plans, 401(k)s are increasingly popular, allowing employees to reduce their salary and thus fund retirement accounts with pretax income.
- Thanks to long-term compounding and employer matching, 401(k) participants can become millionaires by retirement.
- You can feel more comfortable investing in a 401(k) plan that has a provision to make loans to participants.
- When investing 401(k) money, emphasize long-term vehicles such as stock funds and bond funds.
- Don't overload on GICs or your employer's stock.
- In addition to 401(k) plans, take full advantage of flexible spending accounts if offered by your employer.

2 Be Hard-Boiled About Your Nest Egg

How to Handle IRAs, Keoghs, and SEP Plans

The 1981 tax act took an obscure financial term—Individual Retirement Account, or IRA—and made it into a household word. Everybody knew about IRAs and everybody had one.

With good reason. Every working American was entitled to put up to $2,000 into virtually any type of investment or savings vehicle and take a full deduction, year after year. For one-income married couples, deductions could go up to $2,250 a year. Once the contributions were made, the money would grow, tax-free, until withdrawal.

That changed with the 1986 tax act. A clean, simple tax shelter became a study in complexity.

Under the new rules, the limits on IRA *contributions* remain the same. You can put in up to $2,000 a year ($2,250 for one-income couples) and the money will grow, tax-free, until withdrawal.

NOT-SO-ELEMENTARY DEDUCTIONS

The complications result from the rules on what is *deductible*. In essence, if you're not covered by another qualified plan, such as a

401(k) (described in the previous chapter) or a Keogh (to be described), IRAs are fully deductible, up to $2,000 or $2,250.

If you are covered, and if your income is low, you still can get a full tax deduction. If your income is moderate, you might be entitled to a $100 deduction, a $1,000 deduction, or some other number below $2,000 or $2,250. If your income is high and you participate in a qualified plan, none of your IRA contribution will be deductible.

Just to make things even more complicated, the income cut-off points are different for single taxpayers and for those filing joint returns. Moderate income is considered $25,000–$35,000 for single filers, $40,000–$50,000 on a joint return. Planning is difficult, to say the least.

For example, in January 1993, John and Mary Smith each made IRA contributions of $2,000. Bob and Betsy Jones did the same. They all want to start tax-free compounding as soon as possible.

In April 1994, 15 months later, both couples prepare their tax returns for 1993. During 1993, John Smith and Betsy Jones each were active participants in an employer's qualified retirement plan. Therefore, both couples are considered to be covered, for purposes of the IRA deduction.

The Smiths discover they had a pretty good year, with adjusted gross income (AGI) of $46,000. Under the IRA formula, they're entitled to 40 percent of the maximum IRA deduction. (If their AGI turned out to be $47,000, for instance, they'd have a 30 percent deduction, and so on.) Thus, each deducts $800 out of the $2,000 already contributed. Note that the full amount stays in the IRA, compounding free of current taxes—it's only the deductions that are limited.

The Joneses learn they had an even better year, with an AGI of $52,000. Therefore, neither of them qualifies for an IRA deduction. Again, they keep the money in their IRA accounts but they can't claim deductions.

(You can increase the shelter by mixing a 401[k] plan and an IRA. If Betsy Jones had decided to contribute an additional $4,000 to her company's 401[k], the Joneses' AGI would drop from $52,000 to $48,000. Now, both Bob and Betsy would be entitled to a 20 percent, or $400, IRA deduction.)

WITHDRAWAL PAINS

If you think the rules on IRA deductibility are complicated, wait until you take some money out.

Under the old, "everybody deducts $2,000" IRAs, withdrawal rules were simple. Everything you took out was fully taxable; there was a 10 percent penalty tax on withdrawals before age 59-1/2.

Those rules still apply to deductible contributions. Nondeductible contributions, though, are not taxed when withdrawn. Instead, they're treated as a return of your own money.

Now, you might think there's an easy way around this requirement. Your deductible contributions, for example, might all go into a local bank, while your nondeductible contributions all go into a mutual fund. When the time comes, you first make withdrawals from the mutual fund, so you won't owe taxes.

Unfortunately, you can't do it that way. For one reason, as we saw with the Joneses and the Smiths, you can't always know in advance which portion of your IRAs are deductible and which aren't.

But suppose you could tell—you have some old IRAs, which were fully deductible, and now you're sure your IRA contributions will be nondeductible, so they go into a new account. Still, you can't take strictly nontaxable withdrawals.

Whenever you make an IRA withdrawal, you have to make a calculation based on all of your IRA accounts. Whatever the percentage was due to nondeductible contributions, that's the percentage that's sheltered from tax, no matter which account it comes from.

Let's say Rich Worth contributed $10,000 to IRAs at his local bank in the years when IRAs were fully deductible. After the rules changed, he continued to make IRA contributions but, because he's in an employer plan and earns a large income, none of those contributions were deductible. Over the years, he makes $24,000 worth of nondeductible contributions to a mutual fund.

By the time he starts to take money out, the $10,000 he put into the bank has done well, growing to $20,000. The $16,000 that went into the mutual funds did even better, growing to $40,000. Thus, he has a total of $60,000 in his IRAs. Of the total, $16,000 (40 percent) came from nondeductible contributions.

Deductible contributions	$10,000	
Have grown to		$20,000
Nondeductible contributions	$24,000	
Have grown to		$40,000
Total IRA funds		$60,000
Percentage represented by nondeductible contributions		40%

Therefore, when Rich makes his first IRA withdrawal, 40 percent will be a return of his own capital and 60 percent will be taxable. It makes no difference if he takes money out of his bank account, his mutual fund, or some from both.

Just to make matters worse, Rich has to keep track of his nondeductible IRAs in future years. Say, for example, Rich makes a $5,000 withdrawal. Of that $5,000, $2,000 (40 percent) will be a return of capital while the other $3,000 will be fully taxed.

That leaves Rich with $22,000 in his nondeductible IRA "account"—the $24,000 he put in minus the $2,000 he withdrew. Let's say that the IRA account the next year stands at $59,000, after the $5,000 withdrawal and the continued growth of the remaining IRA money. Now, 22/59 of the money in the account is Rich's nondeductible contribution. When he makes another withdrawal, about 37 percent will be untaxed and 63 percent will be taxable.

Rich has to keep these records and make these calculations, year after year. What happens if he doesn't? Unless he can demonstrate the portion relating to a tax-free return of nondeductible contributions, everything he takes out of his IRA will be fully taxed. He'll wind up paying tax on withdrawals of his own money, on which he's already paid tax.

WHY BOTHER?

So making IRA contributions that aren't fully deductible generates uncertainty up front and a paperwork hassle that never quits on the back end. Is it worth it?

Some advisers say it is. The benefits of tax-deferred compounding, long-term, outweigh the aggravation. Besides, putting away

$2,000, year after year, provides needed savings for people who otherwise wouldn't have the discipline.

Such reasoning is questionable, to say the least. If you make a nondeductible IRA contribution, your only benefit is the tax-deferred compounding.

Say you earn 8 percent a year, long-term, on your savings and investments. On $2,000, that's $160 a year. Assuming a 35 percent tax rate (federal, state, local), the tax you're deferring is $56 a year. Remember, the tax is not avoided, just deferred.

It's true that the deferred tax can build if you keep making IRA contributions, to $112 the second year, $168 the third year, and so forth, plus the tax you defer on the investment income. Nevertheless, the benefit seems minor compared with all the required paperwork.

As explained in Chapter 5-9, there are other investments that provide tax-deferred or even tax-exempt income with a lot less hassle. Unless you're a glutton for punishment, skip nondeductible IRAs.

On the other hand, if you qualify to deduct IRA contributions, the tax shelter remains simple and valuable. You should participate up to the $2,000 or $2,250 limit.

CASH IN ON KEOGHS

If you're self-employed or a business owner with only a handful of employees, you can use a Keogh retirement plan. Naturally, if you work as an independent contractor or free lancer or sole proprietor full-time, you're entitled to a Keogh. But, even if you have a part-time or sideline business, you can have a Keogh to shelter some of that income. Like all qualified plans, Keoghs allow you to make tax-deductible contributions; those contributions compound, tax-deferred, until you withdraw funds.

Just as is the case with corporate plans, Keoghs come in two varieties: defined-benefit and defined-contribution. Again, most self-employed individuals choose defined-contribution plans. They're simpler to administer, and they don't lock you in to contributions, good years and bad. Among defined-contribution plans, you have to decide between:

- *Profit-sharing plans.* These plans are favored because of their flexibility—you can contribute as little as nothing in a bad year or as much as 15 percent of compensation, with a $30,000 annual cap. (Because of technicalities, to be explained, the actual cap is around 12.5 percent of self-employment income.)
- *Money-purchase plans.* These plans are more generous because you can contribute 25 percent of your compensation, up to $30,000. However, you must contribute the same fixed percentage of your income each year, or face IRS penalties. (Again, the cap is actually around 20 percent of self-employment income.)

For example, if Maggie Cook works full time as a market researcher for an advertising agency, but also earns $10,000 in a sideline consulting business, she can contribute (and deduct) up to around $1,250 to a Keogh profit-sharing plan. That's in addition to any retirement plan at her full-time job. The next year, if she decides against it, she can skip a contribution to her Keogh plan.

If she chooses a money-purchase plan and elects the maximum contribution, however, she must contribute 20 percent of self-employment income each year.

JUICY PAIRS

If you're willing to make a relatively small commitment, you can have maximum savings along with excellent flexibility. To do so, you establish a "paired" Keogh plan.

In essence, you set up both a profit-sharing and a money-purchase plan. Typically, the money-purchase plan will be structured to accept 10 percent of compensation. That's your fixed commitment.

On top of that, your profit-sharing plan can contribute from zero to 15 percent, as any profit-sharing plan can. So you can contribute as little as 10 percent, in lean years, but up to the 25 percent maximum when times are lush.

Keep in mind that the contribution limits are a percentage of "earned income," calculated as follows:

$$\text{Earned income} = \frac{(\text{Net profits} - 1/2\ \text{Self-Employment tax})}{(1 + \text{Contribution Percentage})}$$

For example, Paul Jones, a free-lance graphic artist, earns $100,000 in 1994, after all business expenses.

Net Profit		$100,000.00
Self-Employment Tax	$8,187	
1/2 Self-Employment Tax		$ 4,093.50
Contribution Percentage	.25	
Earned Income = ($95,906.50) / (1.25)		$ 76,725.20

His maximum Keogh contribution, 25 percent of his earned income, is $19,181.30, or just over 19 percent of his business income.

Therefore, if you agree to contribute 10 percent per year to a money-purchase plan, you're really committing yourself to contribute about 9 percent of your income. Then the profit-sharing plan gives you the flexibility to increase your contribution from 9 percent to around 20 percent.

If you don't care to do the math yourself, prepackaged Keogh plans are available through many banks, insurance companies, and mutual-fund families. Such "fill-in-the-blanks" prototype plans are attractive if you don't need a sophisticated, customized plan design. The mutual fund family T. Rowe Price, for example, offers simplified Keogh plans to sole proprietors, partnerships, and corporations with five or fewer employees.

A PENCHANT FOR PENSIONS

If you're looking for more tax shelter from a Keogh plan, consider a defined-benefit Keogh. As mentioned earlier, defined-benefit plans promise a certain level of retirement income. You can receive as much as you earned at the peak of your career, up to about $115,000 a year in 1993. Each year, the defined-benefit ceiling goes up, indexed to inflation.

Jim Nixon is a self-employed roofing contractor who typically earns $60,000 to $70,000 a year. Therefore, he expects to receive $65,000 a year from his defined-benefit Keogh. When he actually retires and begins to receive his pension, he'll look back and see the three-year period in which he earned the most. His maximum pay-out from the defined-benefit plan will be his average during those three years, up to the current ceiling.

If Jim is planning to receive $65,000 a year in retirement, he'll need a large sum in his retirement account. Depending upon the assumptions, he might need $750,000, $1 million, or even more, to throw off $65,000 each year.

That's the main drawback to a defined-benefit plan. You'll need an actuary to predict your level of retirement income and how much of a nest egg you'll need to build, in order to pay it out. Then, the actuary must predict how much you should contribute each year, in order to reach your goal.

What's more, the assumptions need to be recalculated each year, to factor in differing rates of investment return, different earnings, and so on. For example, if Jim's income shoots up and he becomes eligible for a greater benefit, his annual contribution can increase. But if his investments inside the plan far exceed expectations, his ongoing contributions will decrease, perhaps even disappear.

Naturally, actuaries get paid for making these projections. Start-up costs for a defined-benefit Keogh might exceed $1,000; ongoing fees probably will be less, because it's mainly a matter of plugging in numbers, but they'll still be significant.

In addition to the costs, defined-benefit plans involve more paperwork, more reporting to the IRS. And you're making a commitment to hefty contributions, year after year.

BUILDING A BIGGER PILE, FASTER

With all the expense and aggravation, why establish a defined-benefit plan? Because you may be able to make large contributions, much larger than are possible in a defined-contribution plan.

Suppose that Jim, the roofing contractor who makes about $65,000 a year, has never been able to put any money away. He reaches age 50 with no retirement savings at all.

At this point, though, his circumstances change. For one thing, his kids are finished with their schooling, earning their own living, so Jim's financial commitments are reduced. At the same time, his widowed mother dies, leaving Jim and his sister a modest estate. By the time everything is sold and the proceeds are divided, Jim has over $300,000 in his bank account. Now it's time to think about his own retirement, 15 years away, so Jim sets up a Keogh plan.

If he chooses a defined-contribution plan, he can put in no more than 20 percent of his self-employment income each year, around $13,000. That's what he can deduct.

But he can contribute—and deduct—much more if he establishes a defined-benefit plan. As mentioned, he'll need to build up a huge amount, perhaps $1 million+, in 15 years, if he wants to retire at 65 and receive $65,000 a year in retirement. Depending on the actuarial assumptions, he might be able to contribute $40,000, $50,000 a year, or even more, to a defined-benefit Keogh. (He can't contribute more than he earns, however.)

Notice that Jim can get this deduction by shifting money he already has, from his inheritance, into his Keogh plan, and take a full deduction. Once the money is in the Keogh account, the usual rules apply: taxes are deferred until withdrawal but there's a 10 percent penalty tax on withdrawals before age 59-1/2.

Defined-benefit Keogh plans aren't for everybody. The ideal prospect is someone like Jim, who has substantial self-employment income and is starting relatively late to build up a large amount. Self-employed people in their twenties or thirties won't be able to deduct very much in a defined-benefit plan, so they're better off with a simpler defined-contribution plan.

Even self-employed people sometimes have employees, and they must be covered in a Keogh plan, subject to vesting requirements. If you have a few employees, much younger and lower-paid than you, a defined-benefit Keogh still may make sense. The more employees you have, the older and more highly-paid they are, the more of your defined-benefit dollars will go toward your employees' retirement rather than your own. You may be better off in a defined-contribution plan.

SAFE, SIMPLE, AND SHELTERED

If you're self-employed, or a business owner with a few employees, you may not want to go through the hassle of setting up and maintaining a qualified pension or profit-sharing plan. One alternative is a simplified employee plan (SEP). You get the tax shelter—up-front write-offs, tax-free compounding—without all the paperwork.

You can contribute up to 15 percent of your compensation, but no more than $30,000. Again, complicated calculations bring the maximum contribution to around 13 percent if you're self-employed. Thus, if you earn $50,000 in self-employment income, you can put up to around $6,500 into your SEP each year and take a full deduction.

Unlike some other types of retirement plans, you're not locked into annual contributions. You can put in the maximum one year and make no contribution at all the next year.

If you want, you can exclude employees under age 21 and employees who haven't worked for you in three of the last five plan years. Other types of plans may require contributions for more employees, with shorter histories with your company.

Sometimes, a SEP is known as a SEP-IRA, because you make contributions directly into IRAs, your own and each employee's. In pension-plan lingo, these payments are "portable" and "vested." That is, if employees leave your company, they can take the full amount with them.

SEP MEETS 401(k)

A variation of a SEP plan is a "salary reduction" SEP, known as a SAR-SEP. These plans are comparable to 401(k) plans, but simpler. Again, employees have the option of reducing current income and diverting the money into a tax-deferred retirement plan. SAR-SEPs are limited to companies with up to 25 eligible employees. Workers can choose whether or not to participate, but at least half of all employees must participate for the plan to go into effect.

The maximum contribution goes up each year, indexed to inflation. In 1993, the maximum is about $9,000.

The big advantages to a SEP or SAR-SEP plan are the low cost and the ease of administration. It costs almost nothing to set up a SEP or a SAR-SEP plan while regular qualified plans require thousands of dollars in start-up costs. Generally, annual plan reports needn't be filed with a SEP or SAR-SEP.

If you're a business owner, you naturally want to maximize contributions on your own behalf. However, if a SAR-SEP plan is considered "top-heavy," you, as the employer, have to make contributions for each of your employees, up to 3 percent. To avoid this trap, make sure that "key employees" (owners and others with high salaries) account for no more than 60 percent of total contributions.

If you want to increase your own contribution to a SAR-SEP, but not contributions for employees, you can "integrate" the plan with social security, thus taking into account the social security payments you make for each employee. You might, for example, permit contributions of 3 percent of compensation up to $25,000 a year, then 6 percent of salary over that level. Thus, higher income earners (presumably including you, the business owner) can put more money into the tax-sheltered SEP. Check with your tax pro. Even with these wrinkles, a SAR-SEP will work out to be simpler and cheaper than other kinds of retirement plans you can sponsor for your employees.

SUMMING UP

- IRA contributions no longer are deductible if you have a relatively high income and are covered by an employer plan.
- If you can't make deductible IRA contributions, you can make nondeductible contributions, but the paper-shuffling requirements outweigh the benefits.

- Self-employed individuals can have Keogh plans. A paired plan can give you the maximum write-off of a money-purchase plan plus most of the flexibility of a profit-sharing plan.
- If you're in your fifties or early sixties, a defined-benefit Keogh can boost your tax shelter today and your retirement income tomorrow.
- SEP plans for the self-employed are cheap and easy to administer.

3 Sow Sagely, Reap Richly

Retirement Plan Buildup and Withdrawals

SEPs and 401(k)s and IRAs and Keoghs have one common feature: After the contributions have been made and the deductions have been taken, you direct how the money will be invested. The outcome will determine your level of retirement income. That's a big difference from traditional defined-benefit and defined-contribution plans, where the employer would hire a money manager to make all the investment decisions.

For example, when you opt to participate in a 401(k) plan, you'll be offered several choices. There's usually a stock fund, a bond fund, and a money-market fund, or perhaps several in each category. Other types of retirement plans don't have a "menu" of investments. Instead, you have virtually an unlimited range of stocks, bonds, bank accounts, and mutual funds from which to choose.

With all these choices confronting you, investing retirement-plan money isn't easy. There are, however, rules you can follow to make your life simpler. Essentially, there are two basic strategies to pursue.

ONE BASKET, ALL OF YOUR EGGS

For some people, a retirement plan represents virtually all of their savings. After they get through making their contributions each year, there's nothing left over to save or invest. There might be a few dollars in a bank account, but not much else.

For such people, a retirement-plan account should be looked upon as a total investment portfolio. That is, there should be a mix between stocks, bonds, and cash equivalents. The younger you are, and the more temperamentally able to tolerate risks, the more you should hold in stocks. Long-term, stocks will outperform bonds or cash equivalents. Older, more conservative investors should hold more CDs, bonds, Ginnie Maes, GICs, and other bond-type investments inside their retirement plans.

DIFFERENT STROKES

Your strategy should be different if your retirement plan is only part of your portfolio. Perhaps your income is large enough to permit you to save money in addition to what you put into your plan; perhaps you have received a sizable inheritance that you've invested.

In such cases, there's a simple policy to observe:

- Your least tax-sheltered investments go inside your retirement plan.
- Your most tax-sheltered investments go outside the retirement plan.

Again, you'll want a diversified portfolio of stocks, bonds, and cash. Now, however, the fully taxable investments should be inside your plan. Vehicles such as CDs, corporate bonds, Ginnie Maes, GICs, CMOs, bond funds, foreign bond funds, and so on, enjoy no tax shelter. Thus, they belong in a retirement plan, where the interest can grow, tax-deferred. Similarly, blue-chip stocks that pay sizable dividends can enjoy the shelter of a qualified plan.

At the other end of the spectrum, tax-exempt municipal bonds belong outside of a retirement plan. The same with EE Savings Bonds, on which the tax can be deferred.

Small-cap growth stocks pay low or no dividends, so current taxation isn't a problem: you won't owe the tax until you decide to sell the shares. Therefore, you should hold such stocks outside of a retirement plan. If you sell stocks at a loss, you can take a deduction; inside a retirement plan, trading losses aren't deductible.

What about Treasury bonds? They're subject to federal income tax, so there's an argument for holding them inside a retirement plan. On the other hand, Treasury bond interest is exempt from state and local income taxes. Therefore, investors in high-tax states and cities are wasting a valuable exemption by holding Treasuries inside a retirement plan.

AT RETIREMENT, SHOULD YOU ROLLOVER OR TAKE THE MONEY AND RUN?

Many employer retirement plans give lump-sum distributions: when you leave the company you'll get all your money at one time. If you're in that situation, you're eligible for two tax shelters, but you have to choose one or the other.

One choice is to roll over the sum to an IRA within 60 days. Inside the IRA, your money continues to grow, tax-deferred, so you'll prolong the shelter until you begin withdrawals. Only the money you take out is taxed, leaving the rest of your funds to compound without a tax bite.

What's the downside to this strategy? When you finally take the money out, the amount will be added to your other income and you'll owe tax at your top tax rate (plus a 10 percent penalty tax on withdrawals before age 59-1/2).

LOW-TAXED SPREAD

Your other choice is to take the money without a rollover and pay taxes right away. The shelter here lies in a tax break called "forward averaging." You lose this opportunity if you choose an IRA rollover.

Forward averaging assumes you get the money over a period of years, even though you receive it all at once. Lump-sums start at the bottom of the tax table, rather than on top of your other income. That is, some money is favorably taxed at 15 percent, rather than having the entire sum stacked on top of your earnings and taxed at 28 percent or 31 percent or more.

Suppose you retire in 1994 and receive a $250,000 lump-sum. Ordinarily, that $250,000 would be added to your other 1994 income. Assuming a 31 percent tax rate, you'd owe $77,500 in tax and have $172,500 to reinvest (not counting state or local income tax).

However, if you're at least 59-1/2 and have participated in a retirement plan for at least five years, you're entitled to five-year forward averaging. Thus, you'd have the equivalent of five $50,000 incomes. Each of those incomes would be taxed at 15 percent (on the first $20,000 or so) and 28 percent (on the next $30,000). So you'd owe around $11,000 on each $50,000, or $55,000 in all. Thus, you'd save over $20,000 by using five-year forward averaging.

Even if you use forward averaging, though, all the tax is due the year you receive your money, not over five years.

WHEN 10 IS LESS THAN 5

If you were born before 1936, you have another option: You can use 10-year forward averaging. In our example, that would mean paying the tax on 10 $25,000 incomes. However, you'd have to use the 1986 tax table, which generally has higher rates.

Which works best? In most cases, the break-even point is around $400,000. Lump-sum distributions under that amount are taxed less using 10-year averaging while amounts over $400,000 are taxed less using 5-year averaging.

Should you defer tax with an IRA rollover or cut your taxes with forward averaging? That usually depends on (1) the amount you're rolling over and (2) your need for money. For a rollover of $100,000 or less, you might as well take your money and pay bargain rates of 5 percent to 15 percent.

For larger lump-sums, if you need a large sum right away you're better off with forward averaging. Let's say you want to buy a vacation home, help your children (or grandchildren) with a down payment on a house, or launch a new business. By taking the money now, you'll enjoy the tax break.

| Size of | Effective Tax Rate Using | |
Distribution	10-Year	5-Year*
	Forward Averaging	
$ 20,000	5.5%	7.5 %
$ 50,000	11.7	13.8
$100,000	14.5	15.0
$200,000	18.5	21.4
$300,000	22.1	24.1
$400,000	25.7	25.8
$500,000	28.7	26.9

*Approximate figures based on 1992 tax tables.

But most people need a stream of income in retirement. If you're in that category, you'll wind up with more money using an IRA rollover.

Suppose you retire and receive a $200,000 lump-sum. You're eligible for 10-year averaging. At an 18.5 percent tax rate (see preceding table) you'd owe $37,000. That will leave you $163,000 to invest.

Say you invest that $163,000 and earn 8 percent. Assuming a 31 percent tax rate, you'd net 5.5 percent per year. Then you take out $1,000 per month, $12,000 per year. Your nest egg would last for 25 years.

On the other hand, say you keep your $200,000 in a tax-deferred rollover IRA. Again, you earn 8 percent per year. In the same 25-year stretch, you can take over $1,500 per month (more than $18,000 per year) from your IRA. After tax, assuming that same 31 percent bracket, you'd have around $12,750 per year, so you'd have more retirement income.

TIME YOUR TAX PAYMENTS

What's more, you keep your flexibility with a rollover IRA. If you need a larger amount of cash a few years down the road, you can withdraw what you need and pay only that year's taxes. (Partial rollovers are permitted but any money not rolled over won't qualify for forward averaging. Therefore, you might as well do a full rollover and withdraw money as needed.)

If you expect your retirement income to be modest, so you'll be in a low tax bracket, the IRA rollover will be even more attractive. However, if you expect to be in a top tax bracket, a possible target for rate increases, you might want to take advantage of low-tax forward averaging.

If your lump-sum is over $500,000, you'll gain little by forward averaging. However, a rollover IRA may not be the best choice if you'll run into estate tax or excise tax problems. Anyone with a lump-sum this large should check with a tax pro before making any decisions.

Your state tax situation will have an impact, too. State tax policies vary widely: Some states go along with the federal tax treatment while others don't. Obviously, you're better off with forward averaging if your state complies.

If you plan to move in retirement, probably from a high-tax to a low-tax state, your situation is even more complicated. Some states will go after expatriates to collect taxes on IRA distributions. You might want to use forward-averaging before you move.

A last word on rollovers: The tax law changed, as of 1993, so that your employer must withhold 20 percent of any lump-sum distributions. Unless you handle a rollover correctly, you'll wind up paying tax on that 20 percent, plus a 10 percent penalty tax. What's the right way? Tell your *employer* to transfer the money directly to a rollover IRA. If you don't touch the money, the 20 percent withholding won't apply.

PROLONGING THE ECSTASY

With tax deferral, the longer the better. While your money stays inside your sheltered IRA, SEP, or Keogh, the earnings compound with no tax to impede the growth. As soon as you take it out, you'll owe income tax.

For some people, that's not really a choice. When they retire, they need retirement income more than they need tax shelter. Therefore, they start taking money out as soon as they retire, at 62 or 65 or whenever, and pay the income tax, perhaps in a low bracket.

But that's not always the case. Many people keep working well beyond 65 these days, full or part time, so cash continues to flow in. By that stage in life, some people have inherited sizable estates from their own parents, so they have substantial retirement income. When earned income and investment income are added to social security, there may be enough for a comfortable lifestyle, especially for seniors whose kids are finished with school and whose home mortgages are paid off.

In short, some people don't really need much from their retirement plans. They'd rather keep the money inside the plan as long as possible, extending the tax-free buildup.

Unfortunately, the IRS doesn't have a lot of patience with retirees. There are rules on when to begin withdrawals from retirement plans and how much to take out. If you don't follow the rules, you'll be socked with a 50 percent tax penalty.

A HALF MEANS A WHOLE

The basic rule is that distributions must begin after age 70-1/2. However, the rule is not exactly that basic. For example, people who were born in the second half of the year get a break over people born in the first half.

Take Jane and Joan, lifelong friends and neighbors. Jane was born in January 1924. Therefore, she reaches 70-1/2 in July 1994. According to the rules, she must begin taking money from her retirement plans by April 1 of the following year: 1995.

Joan, though, was born in July 1924. She doesn't reach 70-1/2 until January 1995. According to the tax code, she can defer taking money out until April 1, 1996. Although she was born six months later than Jane, she gets an extra full year of tax deferral.

After they meet their respective April 1 deadlines, both Jane and Joan must continue taking money out, by December 31 of each year.

That is, Jane has two deadlines in 1995, Joan has two deadlines in 1996. After that, they have a full year to take withdrawals.

STRETCHING IT OUT

Figuring "when" to take it out is the easy part; the "how much" is what's difficult. If you take out only $500 when the required minimum is $1,000, you'll owe a $250 penalty: 50 percent of the $500 shortfall.

The simplest, most commonly used technique is the "recalculation method." Each year, you recalculate your life expectancy, according to actuarial tables, and you withdraw the appropriate amount.

For example, if you're 70-1/2, your life expectancy might be 16 years. (Actuarial tables change periodically.) Thus, your first withdrawal must be 1/16 of the total in your retirement plan.

Many people have retirement plans scattered around, in a few IRAs and a Keogh, for example. You don't have to withdraw 1/16 of each plan. Instead, you add up all your plan money and take out 1/16 of the total.

Usually, you'll get statements from your retirement-plan sponsors, giving you the amounts as of December 31. For your first deadline, on April 1, you "look back" 15 months. Otherwise, you look back a year. For example, here's how Joan, who reaches 70-1/2 in January 1995, would calculate her withdrawal:

Payment is due	Based on amount in all retirement plans as of
April 1, 1996	December 31, 1994
December 31, 1996	December 31, 1995
	(less the amount withdrawn by April 1, 1996)
December 31, 1997	December 31, 1996

And so on.

Suppose Joan determines that she has $50,000 in her retirement plans on December 31, 1994. Dividing by 16, she must withdraw at least $3,125 by April 1, 1996. Thanks to the continued tax deferral, Joan might actually have $53,000 or so in her plans by April 1996, but that doesn't matter. As long as she withdraws the required $3,125, she'll be safe from the IRS.

A year later, Joan's life expectancy is a bit shorter, about 15.2 years. On December 31, 1995, she has $52,500 in her plans. If she withdraws $3,125 on April 1, 1996, her effective balance is $49,375. Dividing $49,375 by 15.2 equals $3,248—that's the minimum amount she must withdraw by the end of 1996.

Each succeeding year, she totals up her plan assets on December 31, then makes a withdrawal based upon life expectancy. By the time she's in her eighties, and life expectancy is three years, for example, she'll have to withdraw—and pay taxes on—at least one-third of her retirement-plan money.

The situation is a bit more complex for married couples. If they want, they can use a joint life expectancy, which extends the withdrawal period and prolongs the tax shelter. For example, a 70-year-old husband and a 67-year-old wife have a joint life expectancy of 22 years. They're required to take out only 1/22 of their retirement plan the first year. A year later, with their joint life expectancy at 21.2 years, they'll have to take out 1/21.2 of their balance. And so on.

However, problems arise when one spouse dies. Then the survivor has to recalculate the payout stream based on his or her own life expectancy, and the distribution pace increases sharply.

THAT CERTAIN FEELING

There is a way for spouses to beat this trap. Before the first April 1 deadline, you can elect a "term-certain" payout option. Write to the sponsors of your retirement plans and tell them you will be using this method.

What's the advantage? With a term-certain election, you lock in a withdrawal rate. The first year, a couple with a joint life expectancy of 22 years would have a minimum withdrawal of 1/22 of their balances, 1/21 the second year, 1/20 the third year, and so on. There's no sudden leap in the withdrawal rate when one spouse dies.

Often, term-certain withdrawals provide more tax shelter, deferring the payment of income tax for a longer time period than the recalculation method provides. (If you expect to leave a total estate of well over $600,000, check with your tax pro to see if the benefit of deferring income tax with the term-certain method is outweighed by the potential increase in your estate tax.) However, if either spouse outlives his/her life expectancy, the recalculation method may work out better.

YOUTH MOVEMENT

There's another way to get more shelter out of retirement-plan payouts, especially if you're widowed or divorced. You can choose a joint withdrawal plan, naming a child or grandchild as a beneficiary.

No matter what the age difference, the joint life expectancy will be calculated as if your beneficiary were 10 years younger than you. Obviously, this stretches out the distribution period. If you start at age 70, for example, and name a child as beneficiary, your joint life expectancy is about 26 years. The first year, you need to take out only 1/26 of your portfolio. The next year, it will be around 1/25, and so on.

Best of all (from a tax point of view, at least), assuming you die first, the payout period will be recalculated. For example, if your beneficiary is in her fifties at the time of your death, with a 30-year life expectancy, the first year's minimum distribution is only 1/30 of the remaining balance.

Many banks and brokerage firms, though, are not familiar with the rules. Suppose you name your 25-year-old grandchild as a retirement-fund beneficiary. When you die, these financial institutions often will pressure your grandchild to take out all the money at once—and pay taxes. So you need to be sure your beneficiaries understand their rights.

DIVIDE AND CONQUER

Another tax shelter is particularly useful if you have a large IRA and won't need all the income in retirement. You can transfer the money so that Bank A owns one of your IRAs, Broker B holds another one, Bank C has a third, and so on. You name your spouse as beneficiary of one while your children or grandchildren are beneficiaries of the other IRA accounts.

When you reach age 70-1/2, you'll have to begin taking distributions. Suppose you calculate the minimum distribution you must take as 5 percent of your IRA balances the first year. Instead of taking 5 percent from each IRA, you take the entire distribution from the IRA account where your spouse is the beneficiary.

Each year, you take withdrawals from that account, which shrinks while the others are growing, free of withdrawals. When you die, you'll leave sizable IRA accounts to your children and grandchildren. Then, they can take distributions based on their own life expectancy, perhaps 50 or 60 years. This slows down withdrawals and increases the tax-deferred buildup.

Make certain you write letters to your IRA custodians, stating that you want your IRA beneficiaries to be able to take lifetime distributions. In these letters, you might say that you realize you must make withdrawals based on a combined life expectancy but that after your death your beneficiary can take distributions based on his or her actual life expectancy.

(As another benefit, assets left to children or grandchildren as IRA beneficiaries avoid probate.)

Can you name a minor as an IRA beneficiary? Yes, but you need to do so carefully. Your best bet is to leave the IRA to a trust, naming the minor as trust beneficiary. An adult, probably the minor's parent, should be named as trustee, to receive the IRA payouts.

If you manage your own retirement funds, you can pick the withdrawal method that works best for you. If you participate in an employer plan, however, that may not be so easy: many employers figure distributions solely on the employee's life expectancy, ignoring the beneficiary. If you're in an employer plan, notify your employer before you start to take distributions, listing your beneficiary, his or her date of birth, and your preferred distribution method.

TOO MUCH OF A GOOD THING

This won't be a problem for most people, but there is a 15 percent excise tax on large retirement-plan distributions (generally over $150,000 per year) and large accumulations at death ($750,000). The excise tax is in addition to income and estate tax, so you or your heirs might wind up with only 25 cents on the dollar, after-tax.

If you have a retirement plan this large or you're on your way to building one, check with your tax pro as soon as possible. He or she likely will come up with a strategy (for example, take early distributions close to the $150,000 limit and give the money away) to reduce the tax tab.

SUMMING UP

- If most or all of your savings is in your retirement plan, your plan should be diversified among stocks, bonds, and cash.
- If you have assets outside of a retirement plan, you should hold vehicles with no tax advantages inside a retirement plan.
- Retirees often receive lump-sum distributions from employer plans.
- If the distribution is rolled over to an IRA, no taxes are due immediately. As the money is received, taxes are due at your highest bracket.
- If you choose forward averaging, you'll pay tax now, possibly at lower rates.
- For very small sums, forward averaging is the best choice.
- Forward averaging is best if you need a large sum immediately.
- For delivering a stream of retirement income, a rollover IRA is usually the best choice.

- Retirement-plan distributions must begin after you reach age 70-1/2.
- You can stretch out retirement-plan distributions with a joint withdrawal plan, especially if you name a child or grandchild.
- Large retirement plans are subject to an extra 15 percent tax, which can be avoided or minimized if you work with a first-class tax pro.

4 Putting Your Family First

Permanent Life Insurance as a Triple Tax Shelter

If you have dependents, you need life insurance. Otherwise, how will they manage in case of your untimely death? Congress appreciates this need for life insurance: All life insurance policies qualify for one key tax shelter while some policies get two extra tax breaks.

The tax shelter enjoyed by all life insurance policies is an exemption from income tax. If you take out a $100,000 policy on your life (or a $500,000 policy, or a $1,000,000 policy) and get killed in an auto accident the next week, your beneficiaries will receive the proceeds and owe no income tax.

It makes no difference if you paid just one $100 premium and your beneficiaries receive $100,000 in proceeds. The $99,900 excess is not considered taxable income. (There are some exceptions in case of life insurance policies owned by a corporation, so business owners should consult with a tax pro before buying insurance.)

CASHING IN ON CASH VALUE

To understand the other two tax breaks of life insurance, you need to know a little about insurance. All policies fall into two broad categories: term or permanent. A term policy is nothing more than insurance. You pay a certain premium for coverage for a specific time period, usually one year. After this period, you have the option to renew your coverage, perhaps for another year.

Each time you renew, you're older and your life expectancy is reduced. Therefore, your premium increases with each renewal. This can get to be a real problem when you're in your sixties or seventies and term premiums become incredibly high. If you decide not to pay the premiums then, you're uninsured, no matter how many years you've been paying term premiums.

The solution that insurance companies like to propose is permanent insurance. All the clever names you see advertised—whole-life insurance or universal life or variable life or interest-sensitive life—are all forms of permanent life insurance.

The idea is that you pay much higher premiums than necessary. Instead of paying $200 a year for term insurance, you pay $2,000 a year for permanent insurance. The extra $1,800 goes into an investment account, called the "cash value."

Over the years, you pay a level $2,000 premium and the cash value grows. Even if you reach a point where the term premium exceeds $2,000 a year, you keep paying that same $2,000. The shortfall comes out of your cash value. As long as you pay the annual $2,000, your life insurance is permanent.

There are plenty of variations on permanent life insurance. You might, for example, pay even more upfront so that your premiums "vanish" after 10 years or so but your insurance stays permanent, with premiums paid out of the cash value. But the basic idea of permanent insurance is that you pay excess premiums, building up a cash value account.

That's where the tax shelter comes in. Inside a permanent life insurance policy, the investment income on your premium compounds, tax-free. If, for example, $1,800 of your premium goes into cash value, and that $1,800 earns 5 percent, your cash value grows to $1,890. There's no income tax on the $90 that's earned.

On the other hand, suppose you had invested that $1,800 in a bank account or stock or bond paying 5 percent. Your $90 would be subject to tax and you'd wind up with perhaps a 3.5 percent return.

If you're familiar with the "Rule of 72," you know that

- You divide the investment return into 72.
- The answer is the approximate number of years it takes to double your money.

Dividing 72 by 5 equals 14.4. Thus, if you earn 5 percent a year, your money doubles in around 14 to 15 years. If you hold on for 28 to 30 years, your money will quadruple.

On the other hand, dividing 72 by 3.5 equals 20.5. That's how long it will take for money to double, earning 3.5 percent, after tax. For a quadruple, you'd have to hold on for 41 years. Over that long a time period, you'd have nearly an 8:1 return, at 5 percent.

That's the advantage of tax-free compounding. Over a long time period (40 years), even a slight increase in the average annual return (5 percent versus 3.5 percent) can make a huge difference: an 8:1 return instead of 4:1.

BORROW AND SPEND

Tax-deferred compounding is not the only shelter offered by permanent life insurance. If you need money, you can get it, tax-free.

For example, Samantha Johnson has been paying a $2,000 annual premium for a permanent life insurance policy, building up a cash value of $25,000. Now, her daughter is ready to go to college so Samantha borrows $5,000 from her insurance policy's cash value account. She gets the $5,000 and owes no income tax.

What's more, if Samantha doesn't want to repay the loan, she doesn't have to. As long as she keeps paying the $2,000 annual premiums, the life insurance policy remains in force.

But borrowing against an insurance policy has its costs, too. Interest will be charged, and that interest will compound, as long as the loan isn't repaid. Samantha's $5,000 loan could grow to $6,000, $7,000, or more over the years.

If there is a loan balance at the time of death, the death benefit will be reduced. Suppose Samantha never repays her $5,000 loan and it compounds to $7,000. At her death, her $100,000 policy will pay her beneficiaries only $93,000. That may not be a disaster but, if you borrow too heavily, the policy may collapse. You'll either have to repay loans, pay more premiums, or suffer a policy lapse, which is close to tax suicide: If a cash value policy lapses, all the deferred taxes will come due.

The result is the same—tax-free income, reduced insurance coverage—if Samantha uses partial withdrawals to tap the investment buildup.

There's another tax trap to avoid. If you pay all the premiums up-front, or over a period of a few years, you won't be eligible for tax-free policy loans. (Some people make large premium payments to increase the tax-free compounding.) Just to be safe, you should make relatively equal premium payments over at least seven years. If you don't pass this so-called "seven-pay test," all policy loans or withdrawals will be taxed, up to the amount of your investment income. And there will be a 10 percent penalty on taxable withdrawals before age 59-1/2.

NEVER PAY TAX ON INVESTMENT INCOME

If you put all the life insurance tax breaks together, you can see the ultimate tax shelter for investment income. Take the example of Karen Sanders, a 45-year-old executive. She saves $5,000 a year (10 percent of her income) without crimping her lifestyle.

Instead of putting that $5,000 into the bank, she buys a $250,000 permanent life insurance policy. And, over the next 20 years, she pays a $5,000 premium each year. Her income increases steadily, so that $5,000 becomes easier to save each year.

Over the 20 years, she contributes a total of $100,000 in insurance premiums. She never takes a loan so her cash value increases to $225,000, growing at about 8.5 percent per year.

As you can see, she has deferred taxes on $125,000 in investment income. If she retires at age 65 and cashes in her policy, she'd get back her $225,000, but she'd have a $125,000 taxable gain. Depending on the tax laws at that time, she might owe $50,000, $60,000, or more to the IRS, her state, her city, and so on.

Instead, Karen retires and begins to take policy loans. They're tax-free. If she borrows $20,000, the full $20,000 goes into her pocket, to supplement her other retirement income.

Karen decides to borrow $18,000 a year from her policy. That's 8 percent of her $225,000 cash value. If the remainder of her cash value continues to earn 8 percent, she can continue to take those $18,000 cash distributions indefinitely, and her cash value will remain around $225,000.

Eventually, Karen will die. At that point, depending on several factors, Karen's insurance policy may have a net face value (after policy loans) of $250,000 to $300,000. That amount will go to her beneficiaries, income-tax-free.

What happened to all the tax-sheltered investment interest Karen earned inside the policy? The tax obligation dies along with her. No one ever pays it, yet Karen used her permanent life insurance policy to finance a comfortable retirement lifestyle.

And at the same time, Karen's beneficiaries were protected in case of her untimely death.

This is not to say that permanent life insurance is right for everyone. Permanent insurance is expensive—you need to be able to afford thousands of dollars a year in premiums, in most cases. And you're locked in. If you decide to take money out of a policy in the first 10 years, you generally will find that your money has gone to your agent and the company rather than into your cash value.

But if you have a substantial income and staying power, you may welcome permanent life insurance as a shelter for investment income, especially if you otherwise might not have the discipline to save as much as you'd like to.

MAKE LIFE INSURANCE TAX DEDUCTIBLE

Sometimes the money runs out. Many people have an abundance of needs, even more wants, but not enough cash to pay for everything. For example, you may not have enough money to buy the amount of life insurance you need to protect your family and also fund your retirement plan to the fullest extent possible.

If that's the case, you can let your dollars serve two purposes at once. When you make your contributions to your retirement plan, you can put some of the money into life insurance.

Take the example of George Davis, a successful commercial artist, who's eligible to contribute $10,000 a year into a Keogh plan. He also calculates that he needs $500,000 worth of life insurance to protect his family. If he puts $10,000 into his Keogh plan, he'll have to borrow to buy life insurance, which he doesn't want to do.

Instead, when he puts $10,000 into his Keogh, which he directs, he uses $5,000 to buy a permanent life insurance policy. The other $5,000 is invested in a growth-stock fund. The full $10,000—including the money he used to buy life insurance—is deductible.

The life insurance can be treated as any other insurance policy: George is the insured individual, and at his death the proceeds will go to his wife, named as beneficiary. Thus, George gets tax breaks and family protection. When he reaches retirement age, he can access the cash value built up in the policy via loans or withdrawals.

Now, a tax purist wouldn't recommend this strategy. It's redundant because you're placing one tax-deferred vehicle (permanent life insurance) inside another (a Keogh plan). Technically, you're better off putting taxable investments in the plan and holding life insurance on the outside.

But we live in the real world, not in a textbook. If you have only so many dollars to spend, you may be better off spending them where they can serve two important purposes.

Implementing this strategy is easiest if you direct your own IRA, Keogh, SEP, or small-business retirement plan. However, even if you're an employee participating in a 401(k), you may have a life insurance option into which you can direct some of your contribution.

LIFE INSURANCE AS A RETIREMENT PLAN

On the other end of the spectrum are those with excess dollars. They contribute the maximum to their 401(k) or Keogh or SEP yet they want to build up an even greater retirement fund.

For such people, one strategy is to make large premium payments to a permanent life insurance policy. The cash value will increase; then, you can take policy loans when you need retirement income. You can get at that money, tax-free, while other retirement-plan withdrawals are taxable. In fact, you can tap your insurance policy when you retire at 62 or 65, tax-free, and wait until 70-1/2, when you're legally required to begin taxable withdrawals from your other plans.

ESCAPE ESTATE TAX EROSION

Many sophisticated estate plans include life insurance. There's a natural logic to this: an estate plan takes effect when you die, and that's when life insurance policies pay off. However, there's a huge tax trap for the unwary.

Here, the problem isn't the income tax. Life insurance proceeds generally avoid that tax. Instead, the proceeds may be subject to estate tax, where the rate is much higher than the income tax rate.

For example, you leave a total estate of $1 million, plus a $200,000 life insurance policy. That brings your total estate to $1.2 million. Between $1 million and $1.2 million, the estate tax rate is 41 percent, so your heirs owe an extra $82,000 in estate tax.

In other words, you've paid for $200,000 worth of insurance but your family winds up with only $118,000.

TRUSTWORTHY SOLUTIONS

How can you shelter life insurance proceeds from estate tax? One method is to name your spouse as beneficiary. This works in the short-term, but probably not long-term.

Let's say one spouse dies and the other spouse receives the proceeds, along with other assets. All of those assets escape estate tax. But when the surviving spouse dies, her assets (including the life insurance proceeds) are subject to estate tax. The IRS takes its cut later, but it still takes its cut.

A different approach is to have your kids own your life insurance policy and receive the proceeds. If the policy and the proceeds are outside your estate, no estate tax will be due.

There are a few problems with this approach, though. Your surviving spouse may run short of funds without the insurance proceeds. If the policy is a cash-value policy (common in estate-planning situations), your kids may be tempted to borrow against it, reducing the death benefit. Or, if there's a divorce, the insurance policy may be considered a "marital asset," and some of the cash value may go to an ex-son-in-law or ex-daughter-in-law.

If those are valid concerns, it's worth spending a couple of thousand dollars or so to set up an irrevocable life insurance trust. If the trust owns the policy, it's out of your taxable estate. A properly structured trust can keep the money from profligate children and their disgruntled spouses, too. You can set up the trust to distribute the insurance proceeds to your spouse as well as to your kids. (Or, the insurance money can be used to cover estate tax, leaving other assets intact for your family.)

Setting up an insurance trust isn't a slam-dunk. The IRS frequently tries to include the insurance proceeds in the decedent's taxable estate, particularly if death occurs within three years of the trust's creation. The IRS succeeds when all the niceties haven't been observed, so you have to tread carefully, working with a tax pro.

Your defenses against IRS attack are greatest if you buy a new policy. Set up the trust first and have the trustee make the policy application. Then the trust pays all the premiums. That way, you'll never have any "incidents of ownership" in the policy, so the IRS will be shut out.

If you have an existing policy, you can transfer it to the trust, but you need to work with a tax adviser to avoid incurring a gift tax. Also, you'll have to live for at least three years, to keep the policy out of your estate.

Getting money into the trust, so the premiums can be paid, is another problem only a tax pro can solve. The most common solution is to give money to the trust but allow the beneficiaries a "window" (perhaps 30 days) in which they can withdraw the money you've given. If the beneficiaries have this "Crummey power," named after a court case the IRS lost, then the gift can qualify for the $10,000 or

$20,000 annual gift tax exclusion. If you don't follow the rules carefully, you'll wind up owing gift tax, which can shrink the tax shelter of a life insurance trust.

GET AN INCH, BE LIABLE FOR A MILE

There's another reason to use a life insurance trust: a tax code technicality known as "transferee liability." This obscure rule affected the estate of Gabriel B., a U.S. citizen living in Venezuela. He died there, without a will, so his estate went largely to his widow, a Venezuelan citizen.

The widow refused to pay the estate tax due to the IRS. Therefore, the IRS went after Gabriel's children by a previous marriage. Gabriel had owned a life insurance policy, payable to the children. Because the insurance policy was in his taxable estate, the beneficiaries (his children) were "transferees" of the property, personally liable for all the unpaid estate tax. The Tax Court upheld the IRS position, forcing the children to pay tax on the estate they never received, and left open the possibility that they'd owe interest, too.

Therefore, it pays to keep an insurance policy in a trust and out of your estate.

TWO FOR LESS THAN THE PRICE OF ONE

If you're buying life insurance to cover an estate-tax obligation, rather than to provide for your surviving spouse, consider a "second-to-die" policy. Because these policies won't pay until both spouses die, the premiums are lower than a policy on one spouse. The proceeds can be paid to the couple's children or to a life insurance trust; those proceeds then can be used to pay estate taxes. As long as the policy is not owned by either spouse, the proceeds won't be reduced by any income or estate tax.

Agents often tout second-to-die as a way to "prepay estate tax for 10 cents on the dollar." That is, pay $50,000 in life insurance premiums for a $500,000 policy. The first spouse to die leaves most of his or her assets to his or her spouse, free of estate tax. When the second spouse dies and the $500,000 estate tax bill comes due, the insurance proceeds will be available to cover that expense.

However, the least expensive second-to-die policies are heavy on low-cost term insurance, mixed with a small amount of permanent life insurance. Such policies can turn out to be disastrous as you or your spouse grow older and the term portion becomes increasingly expensive. Be sure there's more permanent than term insurance in a second-to-die policy and be prepared to pay 20 or 30 cents on the dollar in premiums. Still, that's not a bad deal.

An even better deal (financially, at least) is offered by some insurers. If both spouses die within four years of buying a second-to-die policy, they'll pay 222 percent of face value. A $100,000 policy will pay $222,000, for example, at no extra premium. This gives you a year to set up a life insurance trust and three years to pass the (afore-mentioned) IRS challenge period. If the insurer has to pay before the four years are up and the IRS succeeds in including such policies in your estate, you'll be able to pay 55 percent of the proceeds in estate tax ($122,000, in our example) and still wind up with the amount you wanted to buy ($100,000). Manulife Financial and Mutual of New York are among insurers offering this bonus coverage.

MAKE MINE MEC

Before leaving life insurance tax shelters, a word about one that no longer exists: single-premium life. In the mid-1980s, they were extremely popular. You bought a paid-up life insurance policy with one large payment, perhaps $50,000. The money you invested would grow, tax-free. If you ever needed the cash, you could borrow it, tax-free. Who needed CDs?

Single-premium life was so popular that Congress shut the door in 1988. Now, life insurance bought with a single-premium is a modified endowment contract (MEC). The same goes if you buy a policy with a few large payments. If a policy doesn't meet the seven-pay test mentioned earlier, it's a MEC.

As a MEC, life insurance death benefits are still income-tax free and premiums still compound free of income tax. However, the other tax shelter doesn't apply: MECs don't offer tax-free policy loans. Instead, withdrawals are taxable, up to the amount of inside buildup, and there's a 10 percent penalty before age 59-1/2.

In fact, MEC loans and withdrawals are taxed just as loans and withdrawals from deferred annuities are, described in Chapter 7. MECs have a bit less investment buildup, because you're paying for life insurance, but they have a much greater after-tax death benefit. So, if you're in the market for a deferred annuity and you have dependents you'd like to protect, look into buying a MEC instead.

PROCRASTINATORS MAY BE LOSERS

If Congress trimmed the tax benefits on MECs, what are the chances other life insurance benefits will be eliminated? Candidly, not much. The insurance industry is one of the nation's most influential, with well-to-do agents in virtually every congressional district. Moreover, most lawmakers feel that consumers should be encouraged to buy life insurance and protect their dependents.

Still, there may be some limits placed on inside buildup or tax-free policy loans. In the past, any laws affecting life insurance have been prospective rather than retroactive—they haven't restricted policies already sold. So if you buy an insurance policy before any cutoff date announced by Congress, you're likely to lock in the tax shelter.

SUMMING UP

- In most cases, life insurance proceeds are exempt from income tax.
- Permanent life policies offer tax-free investment buildup.
- You can borrow against a permanent life policy's cash value, tax-free.
- By combining these shelters, it's possible altogether to avoid paying tax on investment income.

- Permanent life insurance makes sense only if you can afford to hold the policy 10 years or longer.
- If you can't afford both a full retirement-plan contribution and adequate life insurance, you can make your insurance premiums tax-deductible by buying inside your retirement plan.
- An irrevocable life insurance trust can shelter life insurance proceeds from estate tax.
- Second-to-die policies are relatively inexpensive because they pay after two people die.
- A modified endowment contract may appeal to people interested in investing in annuities, if they have dependents.

5 Mastering the Muni Maze

Shelter Investment Income with Tax-Exempt Bonds

Fool me once, shame on you. Fool me twice, shame on me. That's an old refrain, but here's the updated version:

Tax me once, shame on you. Tax me twice, shame on me.

In other words, there's not much you can do about paying tax on income you earn. But after you earn that income and pay the income tax along with all your other expenses, you may have some money left over to invest. Naturally, you hope to earn something—interest or dividends or capital gains—on your investments. But why pay tax again on those earnings when you don't have to?

One way to avoid tax on investment income is to buy municipal bonds. Like all bonds, they pay interest. The interest, though, is exempt from federal income tax.

The word "exempt" is not to be taken lightly. That means no tax is due, ever. With other types of investments, the taxes are deferred, which means they'll have to be paid later.

A LITTLE HELP FROM OUR FRIENDS

The term "municipal" bonds is a misnomer because they're issued not only by municipalities but also by states and by all kinds of local government agencies. To help these agencies raise money, Congress has granted their obligations tax-exempt status. As a result, they can pay lower interest rates.

For example, suppose AT&T wants to issue long-term bonds. Because of current market conditions, it has to pay 9 percent interest.

Let's say the state of Illinois wants to issue long-term bonds at the same time. If it is just as creditworthy as AT&T, it also should pay 9 percent interest.

However, the bondholder who buys AT&T bonds will owe federal income tax on the interest earned. Instead of 9 percent, he'd end up with around 6 percent, after-tax.

On the other hand, bonds issued by the state of Illinois are considered municipals, or munis, so the interest is tax-exempt. Thus, the state of Illinois might offer to pay, say, 7 percent interest. The Illinois bondholder won't pay anything to the IRS, so he'll keep 7 percent, after-tax.

- The investor comes out ahead, netting 7 percent instead of 6 percent.
- The state of Illinois comes out ahead, paying 7 percent interest instead of 9 percent.

Who loses? The IRS, because it collects no tax on municipal bond interest. But Congress has decided that this revenue loss is worth giving up, on the federal level, so that states and local governments will have an advantage in borrowing money.

The higher income tax rates go, the more valuable the tax shelter from municipal bonds (if you're in a 15 percent tax bracket, don't buy munis). Despite the drain on federal revenue, the political support for munis is so great that there is little chance Congress will substantially trim this tax shelter.

RISKY BUSINESS

So far, investing in munis sounds pretty straightforward. You invest in bonds, collect tax-exempt interest with no fears of an IRS audit, and get your money back at maturity. But that's just the beginning: Munis have risks, which you should know about before investing.

One risk is called market risk. That is, if you sell a bond before redemption, there's a risk you might sell at a lower price than you paid, taking a loss.

If you buy a bond maturing in a year, market risk is scant. The bond will be redeemed soon, at full price, so it's not likely to vary much from that price. If you want to sell, you'll be able to find a buyer who'll pay close to the redemption price.

The longer the time until maturity, the greater the market risk. Sometime in the next 20 or 30 years, interest rates might shoot up, and rising interest rates always lower bond prices. (An old 8 percent bond is less attractive if investors can earn 12 percent on a new bond.)

Long-term bonds generally have higher interest rates than short-term bonds, to make up for the increased risk. Investors, therefore, have to make a tradeoff: How much market risk are they willing to accept (How long will you wait for a bond to mature?), in return for a higher yield?

DEFAULT LINES

A similar tradeoff is necessary when evaluating another type of risk: default risk. Some bond issuers are rock-solid, certain to pay all the promised interest and return your principal. Other bond issuers are shaky, so there's a real risk you won't get all you were promised. There were, in fact, billions of dollars of defaults in the municipal bond market in the 1980s and early 1990s.

The most creditworthy municipal bonds often receive AAA or AA ratings from agencies such as Moody's or Standard & Poor's or Fitch Investors Service. Bonds that are not as solid get A ratings, B ratings, and so forth. And many munis aren't rated at all—the issue is so small that it doesn't make sense to pay for a rating.

Again, the difference in financial strength is reflected in the bond yields. An AAA-rated muni likely will have a lower yield than a B-rated bond or an unrated bond.

There are special factors that go into determining a rating for a municipal bond. Some munis are general obligation (G.O.) bonds, meaning that they're backed by the taxing power of the issuer. If an Illinois G.O. bond, for example, is in danger of default, the state can increase taxes to repay the debt. Revenue bonds, on the other hand, are backed only by one specific project. A revenue bond issued to build moderate-income apartments might be supported by the rentals from those units. If the apartments have too many vacancies, or if rent levels are lower than predicted, bondholders might be hurt.

Therefore, G.O. bonds are usually rated higher than revenue bonds. If you're interested in the ratings on a particular bond, S&P (212-208-1723) and Fitch (800-753-4824) will send free copies of research reports to investors who call.

WORST OF BOTH WORLDS

Another type of risk faced by muni investors is call risk. Suppose you buy a 20-year muni for $1,000. The issuer might have the right to repurchase the bond at par ($1,000) or even slightly above par, after 5 or 10 years, for example.

So what's the risk here? Bonds, as noted earlier, rise in price when interest rates fall and fall in price when interest rates rise. A call provision sticks the buyer with a heads-you-lose, tails-you-don't-win dilemma.

Let's take the case of Mindy Owens, who buys a $1,000, 20-year muni from the North Shore Water Treatment District, an extremely creditworthy issuer. The coupon is 8 percent, so she receives $80 in interest each year, tax-exempt.

Ten years from now, interest rates have shot up to 10 percent, so investors can earn $100 per year per $1,000 bond. Her old bond, then, is devalued, worth only $800. If she wants to sell, she'll take a loss.

Suppose, on the other hand, interest rates have fallen to 5 percent. Now, investors can get only $50 per year per $1,000 bond. Her 8 percent bond, paying $80 a year, is worth more—it should be worth $1,600.

However, her bond has a call provision. North Shore, tired of paying 8 percent interest, calls in the bonds and issues new ones, paying 5 percent. For North Shore, the call provision saves millions of dollars.

For Mindy, though, the call feature is not so favorable. Nobody will buy her $1,000 bond for $1,600, which should be the market price, because the bond will soon be called for $1,000. The bond likely will trade around $1,000 as it nears the call date. After her bond is called, she'll get her money back and have to reinvest in a low-rate environment.

So Mindy can lose if interest rates rise, but she won't gain if interest rates fall. Bond calls truly present investors with a no-win proposition.

From another point of view, suppose Stan Harris, a novice investor, buys Mindy's bond for $1,300. He's delighted with the idea of getting a bond that would be worth $1,600 at this low price. In a 5 percent world, he's earning over 6 percent, tax-exempt:

He buys Mindy's bond for	$1,300
The annual bond interest is	$ 80
The current interest rate is	6.15%

A year later, though, the bond is called in at $1,000. Stan winds up with a $300 loss (23 percent on his $1,300 investment).

SQUEEZE PLAYS

Muni investors have yet another risk to contend with—the risk of dealing in inefficient markets.

Municipal bonds aren't traded on an exchange. There are virtually no quoted prices to follow in the daily newspapers. Instead, each bond transaction is one of a kind, at a price quoted by the broker. Often, there are large disparities from broker to broker.

In 1992, a *Wall Street Journal* reporter called several muni bond dealers, asking for quotes on bonds with a face value of $10,000. The quoted prices were all different, ranging from $9,500 to over $9,800. An institutional seller, the article implied, might have sold the bonds at an even higher price. Individual investors, though, are often treated as prey by bond brokers.

Altogether, investing in munis offers land mines as well as the lure of tax-exempt interest. Unless you really know the ins and outs of the market, stick with top-rated (AA or better) munis. Keep your maturities to 10 years or less.

One super-safe strategy is to hold municipal bonds maturing in two, four, six, and eight years. Every two years, as your bonds mature, you can reinvest in eight-year bonds. This will reduce your market risk yet give you decent tax-exempt yields.

LOCAL HEROES

Munis, as mentioned, are exempt from federal income taxes. That exemption, however, doesn't apply to state or local income taxes. For example, let's say Mindy lives in a state where she has a 10 percent income tax.

She bought a municipal bond for	$1,000
At 8 percent, her annual interest income is	$ 80
Her federal income tax is	0
Her state income tax ($80 x 10 percent)	$ 8
So her after-tax income is ($80 - $8)	72
On a $1,000 investment, her after-tax yield is	7.2%

As an alternative, Mindy could have bought a bond issued in her home state. In-state municipal bonds are "double tax-exempt," free of state income tax as well as of federal tax. Some munis are "triple tax-exempt," avoiding local income tax as well.

Naturally, Mindy would rather earn 8 percent on an in-state bond than 7.2 percent on an out-of-state bond. Even if the in-state bond pays only 7.5 percent or 7.6 percent, she's better off.

But if she loads up her portfolio with in-state bonds, she runs the risk that her bonds will lose value if her state runs into economic distress. Just ask Massachusetts, New York, and California bond-holders what happened to them in the late 1980s and early 1990s.

So Mindy has to make a choice: higher yield versus more risk. If she's comfortable about her home state's economic prospects, or if she's certain she can hold onto her bonds until maturity, she's probably better off buying in-state bonds and earning the higher after-tax yields, year after year. But if she thinks she may have to sell before the bonds mature and she wants to reduce her risk of a capital loss, she's better off with a geographically diverse portfolio of bonds, paying state tax on the interest.

SAY UNCLE

There's a better way to stretch for yields in the muni market, without locking yourself into your home state's economic performance. You can buy "prerefunded" or "pre-re" bonds. In essence, these are tax-exempt municipal bonds backed by super-safe Treasury bonds.

But munis and Treasuries are two different types of investments—how do the twain come to meet? To understand, take the example of bonds issued by Jacksonville, Florida, back when interest rates were relatively high. These bonds have a coupon of 7-3/4 percent. That is, for every $10,000 invested at the initial offering, bondholders receive $775 a year, tax-exempt. On the flip side, Jacksonville has to pay $775 per year, per $10,000 outstanding.

Since the bond issue, interest rates have declined. Jacksonville would like to issue low-interest bonds, replacing the high-coupon bonds, but the bonds can't be called until October 1995. If Jacksonville waits until then to refinance, bond yields may have rebounded, increasing Jacksonville's cost.

Therefore, Jacksonville issued new bonds in 1992, when its officials thought yields were at or near their lows. With the money raised from the new bond issue, Jacksonville bought Treasury bonds and put them in escrow. At the first call date (October 1995, in our example), the Treasuries will be used to redeem the old bond issue.

Jacksonville, then, locks in 1992's low costs of borrowing. Investors, moreover, can buy the old bonds with virtually no risk of default. The pool of Treasuries guarantees repayment. Because the bonds will be redeemed in a few years, there's little interest-rate risk, as well.

So pre-res are as safe as munis can be. Yet they have higher yields, too. How can this seeming paradox be explained?

Remember, bonds that are candidates for pre-res are high-coupon bonds. They pay interest that's above the market rates. Because they pay such high rates of interest, they trade at a premium. A $1,000 bond might trade at $1,050, $1,100, or even more. In 1992, the Jacksonville pre-res were trading at $1,110 per bond, yet they were callable in 1995, at $1,020 per bond. So here's what investors were looking at:

To buy $10,000 (face value) worth of bonds cost	$11,100
These bonds will likely be redeemed in 1995 for	$10,200
There's a built-in loss of	($900)

Few investors willingly will invest over $11,000 for a certain $900 loss. Moreover, under the tax law, such a loss won't be deductible.

But look at the upside. With a 7.75 percent coupon, the bondholder will collect $775 per year, or $2,325 over three years, in tax-exempt interest. Even after factoring in a $900 loss, the investor's net gain is $1,425 over three years. That's a compound yield of around 4.2 percent per year, tax-exempt.

By comparison, if that same investor had bought $10,000 worth of conventional munis, maturing or callable in October 1995, the total return would have been around $1,200, for a compound after-tax yield of 3.9 percent.

	Pre-Re	Conventional
Three-year total return	$1,425	$1,200
Compound after-tax yield	4.2%	3.9%

In addition to the higher returns, pre-res are just about free of default risk, so they're safer than conventional munis. They're ideal for low-risk investors who want tax-exempt income. Most brokers who sell munis also handle pre-res.

DON'T CALL FOR COPS

If pre-res are higher-yield munis that are super safe, COPs are higher-yield munis that are super risky. For most investors, the slight extra yield you get from COPs is not worth the extra risk.

COP is an acronym for "certificates of participation." They have become very popular in the 1990s as taxpayer opposition to new taxes and new bond issues increased. COPs are a vehicle enabling politicians to borrow money without first getting voter approval.

In essence, the borrowed money is used to buy various items on a "lease-purchase" basis. Each year, the government body appropriates money to pay off these installment purchases. The payments go to the COP holders, partly as a return of principal and partly as tax-exempt interest.

The weakness here is that COPs are not really long-term obligations on the part of the borrower. Instead, there must be an appropriation each year. If the government decides to skip the appropriations, the COP holders receive no payments. Their only recourse is to seize the property or the equipment that the COPs bought.

For a real-life example of when COPs turn into robbers, consider what happened in Brevard County, Florida. Without a popular vote, the county's Board of Commissioners issued COPs to fund construction of a county office building in 1989. Within a couple of years, the people in the county expressed unhappiness with having to travel to the new building and for having to pay for it. In early 1993, a referendum was held, and use of the building was narrowly approved. If the vote had gone the other way, Brevard County would have stopped making annual appropriations for lease payments, and COPs investors would have stopped receiving those payments.

Nor was Brevard County the only place where COPs borrowers considered copping out. Before that, several COPs issues in California went into default; after the Brevard incident, other COPs issuers threatened to cease making yearly appropriations.

In default situations, the COP holders usually can foreclose, but how much value is there in an empty government office building or a used fire truck?

Therefore, COPs really aren't for individual investors, even though you might get an extra 0.25 percent or 0.5 percent in yield. However, if you work with a broker whose firm specializes in COPs research, you might invest modestly. A first-class analyst will be able to tell whether the assets purchased are truly vital to the user, whether an enforceable no-substitution clause is in place, and so on. But proceed cautiously and invest only if you're confident that the annual appropriations will continue.

SURE THINGS

Fortunately for the investors in the Brevard government office building, the COPs were insured. That is, the Municipal Bond Insurance Association (MBIA), a pool of private insurance companies, had agreed to step in if the issuer defaulted. Therefore, the investors were sure to keep on receiving interest and principal from MBIA, which seized the collateral (the building) to try and recoup its outlays.

Municipal bond insurance is widespread these days. Among several major insurers, the leaders are MBIA and American Municipal Bond Assurance Corp. (AMBAC), a private corporation. In most cases, the issuer buys the insurance policy.

Insured munis generally get a top rating (AAA) because both the issuer and the insurance company stand behind the bond. They're considered extremely safe for investors, not only because of the extra layer of protection but because insured bonds have passed the insurance company's scrutiny. After all, no insurer is eager to back bonds that will go into default.

For investors, the yield is slightly lower than the yield on uninsured AAA bonds, because the cost of insurance usually is passed through. Nevertheless, many investors will settle for an 0.1 percent or an 0.25 percent lower yield in return for the added safety.

TOO GOOD TO BE TRUE

At the other end of the spectrum are some unrated munis that are incredibly high risk. Why would tax-exempts issued to buy the Dearfield Nursing Home in Columbus, Georgia, yield 10 percent in 1993 while top-ranked munis pay 6 percent? Because the nursing home had been losing money for years, struggling to keep up its interest payments since they were issued in 1989. According to *Forbes* magazine, only a last-minute payment of property tax averted a sheriff's sale in early 1993.

Similarly, an unrated offering for Liberty Manor, a nursing home in Midway, Georgia, reportedly showed that the project would lose money even at a 98 percent occupancy rate. So don't buy unrated munis, especially if you hear about them from phone salespeople who call to offer you super-high yields, tax-exempt.

SUMMING UP

- Interest on municipal bonds is exempt from federal income tax.
- The higher your tax bracket, the greater the tax shelter from munis.
- Munis are subject to many types of risk, so your best choice generally is to buy short-term, top-rated munis.
- If you're certain you can hold until maturity, you can increase your after-tax yield with locally issued munis, which are exempt from state and local income tax, too.
- For extra safety, you can buy insured munis or prerefunded munis backed by Treasury bonds.
- Individual investors should stay away from COPs and from unrated munis, especially if they're pitched to you on the phone by an unknown broker touting high yields.

6 These Guns for Hire

Professional Management for Your Municipal Bonds

As explained in the previous chapter, investing in munis is no slam-dunk. You have to choose among all the different issues out there, deciding on maturities and credit quality and in state versus out of state and insured versus uninsured bonds and exotic munis such as COPs. For most people, choosing intelligently among all the possibilities is impossible, so they ask their broker for advice on tax-exempt bonds. Most brokers, in turn, are only too happy to make recommendations; generally, those recommendations just happen to be whatever the broker's firm has on the shelf at that moment.

There are other ways to invest in munis—through managed accounts. You can hire a professional who follows the market full time to select a portfolio of munis for you. If you can afford to own hundreds of thousands of dollars worth of munis, a professional money manager will buy a customized bond portfolio on your behalf. For most investors, though, the most practical way to hold munis is through some type of a public fund.

BUY 'EM AND HOLD 'EM

Among funds, the simplest is called a unit investment trust, or merely a unit trust. Such unit trusts are formed continually by

61

well-known firms such as John Nuveen, Van Kampen Merritt, and others.

Each muni bond unit trust raises a certain amount of money and buys an assortment of munis selected by the managers. A $20 million unit trust might invest in a dozen different issues, buying $1 million to $2 million per issue. Typically, unit trusts buy long-term bonds.

And that's it. The unit trust holds onto its original bonds, year after year. It collects the interest and pays it out to the unit trust investors. As for the investors, they receive a fixed payout, year after year.

With unit trusts, the main advantage and the disadvantage are one and the same: You lock in one yield for the life of the trust. If you had invested when muni yields were 8 percent or 10 percent, for example, you'd keep collecting that 8 percent or 10 percent until the bonds are called or redeemed. Obviously, that's attractive when muni bonds yield 6.5 percent or 7 percent, as they did in early 1993.

On the other hand, you're taking a risk when you lock in muni yields of 6.5 percent for the life of the trust, which might be 20 years or more. That 6.5 percent won't look so appealing if inflation rebounds to 7 percent a few years from now and municipal bonds pay 10 percent. Generally, the time to buy unit trusts is when bond yields are at or near their cyclical peak. In 1993, with bond yields at 20-year lows, investing in unit trusts made little sense.

CUT-RATE CLOSED-ENDS

Besides unit trusts, another way to hire a municipal bond manager is to invest in a closed-end fund. A closed-end muni fund actually begins life like a muni unit trust. Millions of dollars are raised from investors, who generally contribute a few thousand dollars apiece. The money that's raised is used to buy a diverse portfolio of municipal bonds, selected by a pro. Investors receive shares in the fund.

Unlike a unit trust, a closed-end fund trades like a stock, commonly on an exchange. For example, the John Nuveen Select Tax-Free Income Fund 2, traded on the New York Stock Exchange, sold anywhere from $13.50 to $15.25 a share in 1992.

In another contrast to unit trusts, closed-end funds are actively managed. If the fund's manager is worried about a particular bond in the portfolio, it can be sold and replaced with another. Depending on circumstances, maturities can be increased or decreased, troubled issuers can be supplanted, and so on. You can't do that with a unit trust.

Because they're actively managed, closed-end funds are similar to the mutual funds with which you're probably familiar. However, closed-ends tend to be smaller and they're closed to new investors; hence the name.

There's a unique factor involved in investing in closed-end funds. Once funds trade on an exchange, like common stocks, the prices are determined by supply-and-demand. Those prices may be more or less than the value of the underlying municipal bonds, the net asset value (NAV) per share.

Muni Closed-End Fund A owns municipal bonds worth	$100 million
The number of outstanding shares is	20 million
Each share thus has an NAV of ($100 million/20 million)	$5

If Muni Closed-End Fund A sells for $5.50 a share, it trades at a 10 percent premium to NAV. If this fund sells for $4.50 a share, it trades at a 10 percent discount to NAV. In practice, most closed-end funds trade either above or below NAV.

At the end of 1992, for example, Nuveen Select Tax-Free Income 2 had a net asset value of $14.46 per share. The fund was trading at $13.625 per share. Thus, if you bought 100 shares then, you would have acquired $1,446 worth of municipal bonds for $1,362.50. That's a discount of 5.8 percent.

Buying bonds at a discount increases your yield. The Nuveen fund mentioned here, for example, was paying 6.66 percent, at a time when the Bond Buyer index of municipal bonds showed a 6.45 percent yield. Investors get high yields along with diversification and professional management.

Nevertheless, picking a closed-end muni fund isn't easy. There are dozens of such funds, and each is slightly different from the others. In late 1992, for example, you might have bought Seligman Quality Municipal Bond Fund, with a yield of 6.64 percent, or American Municipal Term Trust II, with a yield of 6.05 percent. The difference? The Seligman fund had an average maturity of nearly 27 years, so you'd have a great exposure to interest-rate increases, while the American fund had a 10-year maturity and much less interest-rate risk.

At the same time, Putnam Investment Grade Muni Fund was paying 7.31 percent. To get this high yield, the Putnam fund was 56 percent invested in bonds rated A, BBB, BB, or lower. By contrast, the Seligman fund, with its 6.64 percent yield, was 81 percent invested in AAA munis.

Some closed-end funds are structured to produce even higher yields. Colonial Municipal Income Trust, for example, is sold as a "high-yield" muni fund. In late 1992, its yield was 8.34 percent. How? By investing 66 percent of its portfolio in unrated (and presumably more risky) municipal bonds.

Yet another class of muni closed-end funds hold bonds from one state, to provide state tax relief, too. Nuveen California Municipal Value Fund, for example, was yielding a modest 6.2 percent in late 1992, but that yield was net of state and federal tax.

Moreover, most closed-end municipal funds have some exposure to the alternative minimum tax (AMT). Some munis issued for "private purposes" (for example, housing projects) are subject to the AMT, which is a complex subject requiring extensive calculations. The end result is that some investors, if they have a great deal of tax deductions and credits, will wind up owing federal income tax on the interest from AMT munis and therefore on the interest from many closed-end bond funds.

BORROW SHORT, LEND LONG

If you're interested in closed-end bond funds, there's yet another wrinkle you need to know about. Some funds use leverage. That is, they borrow and use the borrowed money to buy more bonds.

In most cases, the funds sell renewable preferred shares maturing in 7 days or 28 days. Every 7 or 28 days, the investors can either redeem their preferred stock or roll it over at the current rate. In early 1993, such preferred shares were yielding around 3 percent. That is, some closed-end funds issued short-term paper to investors who were willing to accept 3 percent yields on low-risk, tax-exempt vehicles.

The closed-end funds then invested that money in long-term munis, paying 6 percent or 7 percent or whatever. If a fund borrows at 3 percent and invests at 6 percent, it will have excess interest to distribute to the investors holding common shares, those traded publicly. Using leverage can add around a point of interest income, so most closed-end munis use leverage.

Using leverage increases risks: That's the flip side of increasing yield. As long as short-term rates are low, leverage works. Borrowing at 3 percent and lending at 6 percent is a sure road to riches. But what happens if interest rates go up and the preferred stock rolls over at 4 percent, 5 percent, even 6 percent or higher? Your fund will have to pay higher yields on the preferred stock, but it's locked into the 6 percent yield on the long-term bonds it purchased. Interest income will fall and even disappear, in a worst case. Investors may be hit with huge capital losses.

Generally, muni closed-ends that buy lower-rated bonds and single-state muni closed-ends don't use leverage. Those funds have enough risks for investors without adding leverage, too.

FEELING MUTUAL

The third path to owning a managed portfolio of municipal bonds is through traditional open-end mutual funds. Here, the selection difficulty is even more difficult: In early 1993, there were more than 500 mutual funds that hold municipal bonds, over 20 percent of all the mutual funds on the market.

With this assortment, there are mutual funds for almost any taste. As of this writing, there are more than 100 funds for California or New York investors, plus another 220 funds for other states. Local investors can avoid all income taxes with these funds.

Yet another 200 mutual funds hold munis issued throughout the United States. With those funds, your interest will be exempt from federal income tax but subject to state and local income taxes.

Not only can you choose in-state versus national muni funds, you also can select maturities. The USAA family, for example, offers a short-term fund with an average maturity of 3 years, an intermediate fund with an average maturity of 8 years, and a long-term fund with a 21-year average maturity. Vanguard offers, among others, a "short-term" muni fund with a one-year average maturity and a "limited-term" muni fund with a three-year average maturity. There also are "vanilla" muni funds with high-grade bonds and high-yield muni funds that buy low-rated bonds.

What should you look for in a mutual fund? If you buy a no-load mutual fund, you can cut out the broker's fee, raising your return. Look for a fund with annual expenses under 75 basis points [0.75]. A good manager will earn that much for you with active management. Mutual funds must publish their expense ratios.

In early 1993, investors generally were better off buying short- and intermediate-term muni funds. Many muni funds were chasing after long bonds, driving up prices there. Therefore, the yields on 30-year munis were barely higher than the yields on 15-year bonds. Investors were not being paid for the risks they'd have to take.

If those are the criteria—no sales load, average maturity under 15 years, expense ratio under 75 basis points—which muni funds hold up well? Here are the funds that met or approached those standards and received five stars in early 1993 from Morningstar, which rates mutual funds:

- Federated Short-Intermediate Municipal Fund
- Scudder Medium-Term Tax-Free Fund
- Sit "New Beginning" Tax-Free Income Fund
- USAA Tax-Exempt Intermediate-Term Fund
- USAA Tax-Exempt Short-Term Fund
- Vanguard Municipal Limited Term Fund
- Vanguard Municipal Short-Term Fund

Does it pay to buy a single-state muni fund and thus avoid state and local income tax? Probably not. You're too exposed to downturns in the state's economy. In addition, most single-state muni funds are long-term, so there's considerable market risk.

Considering those risks, the extra returns aren't that great. None of the single-state funds ranked five stars by Morningstar in early 1993 met all of the criteria mentioned here.

The single-state five-star fund that came closest was Fidelity Massachusetts Tax-Free High-Yield. The average maturity was just under 20 years. Therefore, the most comparable national muni fund on the list is Sit New Beginning, with an average maturity of around 17 years.

If a Massachusetts investor were to buy the Sit fund, then yielding 6.6 percent, and pay the state's top tax rate of 12 percent, the net yield would be 5.8 percent.

Fund yields	6.6%
Federal tax	0
State tax @ 12% (6.6% x 0.12)	0.8%
Net after-tax yield to Massachusetts investors	5.8%

By comparison, the Fidelity Massachusetts fund paid 6.2 percent. So the investor who bought the single-state fund, exposed to the Massachusetts economy, earned an extra 0.4 percent, or $100 a year on a $25,000 portfolio. That's scant reward for the added risk.

The shortest-term single-state fund on the Morningstar list was Benham California Tax-Free Intermediate-Term Fund, with an average weighted maturity of 7.5 years, which rated three stars from Morningstar.

Five-star national funds with comparable maturities, from Scudder and USAA, were yielding 6 percent, so a California investor in a top 10 percent bracket would net 5.4 percent—actually a smidgen higher than the lower-rated, single-state Benham fund, which paid 5.3 percent. Unless you're a fanatic about avoiding taxes, you're best served in a top-rated national muni fund.

SHORT-SHORTS

In addition to the hundreds of muni mutual funds already mentioned, there also are hundreds of tax-exempt money market funds. These are mutual funds that hold extremely short-term municipal paper; typically, the average maturity is less than two months.

Because there's virtually no market risk, tax-exempt money funds are like ordinary money funds. The price per share stays at $1 and never fluctuates, so you won't suffer a capital loss. The interest you receive is tax-exempt and, unless you request distributions, is automatically added to your account balance.

Unfortunately, low-risk money market funds are low-yield. In early 1993, the average yield on tax-exempt money funds was only 2 percent. Investors probably were better off going out a few years in average maturity, where they could earn 4 percent to 5 percent from short-term muni funds.

OPEN OR CLOSED?

Compared with muni mutual funds, closed-end muni funds tend to offer higher yields. To get those higher yields, though, they have to take risks: They use leverage or they buy long-term bonds or AMT bonds or low-rated bonds. If high tax-exempt yields are extremely important to you and you're willing to take some risks, closed-ends may be suitable.

If you're a more conservative investor, though, you'd probably prefer an open-end mutual fund with high-grade, short- to intermediate-term munis. True, yields on high-quality mutual funds will be relatively modest. In early 1993, when closed-end munis were paying 6 percent to 8 percent, short- and medium-term national muni mutual funds were paying 4.5 percent to 6.5 percent. You have to decide whether you want to play it safe, and receive lower yields, or shoot for higher yields with riskier funds.

SUMMING UP

- Because investing in municipal bonds is so risky, you may prefer to buy through a professionally managed fund rather than to buy your own individual bonds.

- One type of fund is a unit investment trust, which provides a fixed return over a period of years. However, when interest rates are low, you may not want to lock in yields through unit trusts.

- A second alternative is to invest in a closed-end fund, which holds a variety of munis yet trades like a stock.

- Closed-end muni funds often pay high yields. However, to deliver those yields they have to take risks, such as using leverage or buying long-term or unrated bonds.

- There are hundreds of open-end muni mutual funds from which to choose, offering convenient investing as well as access to your money.

- Your best choices among muni funds are no-loads with low expense ratios holding national portfolios.

- To reduce your risk, buy muni funds where the average portfolio quality is AA or better and the average maturity is around 15 years or less.

7 Better Later

Supplement Your Retirement Income with Deferred Annuities

The U.S. economy struggled in the late 1980s and early 1990s, but that didn't have much impact on sales of annuities. From 1989 to 1992, assets in annuities more than tripled, with some reports putting the total in the hundreds of billions of dollars. What was the big attraction? Relatively high yields, tax deferred.

In early 1993, for example, most bank CDs were paying 3 percent to 4 percent. Annuities, at that time, were generally paying around 7 percent. Moreover, interest on bank accounts is immediately taxable while annuity interest may be deferred, perhaps for decades.

As of this writing, it seems certain that income tax rates will rise in the 1990s. Higher tax rates make tax deferral more valuable, so deferred annuities may become a better investment in the coming years. But before you rush out to buy an annuity, you need to know what they are and how they work.

GIVE AND TAKE

A basic annuity is a contract between two parties, with one guaranteeing the other a certain income stream. For example, you retire and

71

your employer agrees to pay you $1,000 a month for the rest of your life, as part of the company's pension plan.

Investors can get this kind of deal by purchasing an *immediate annuity*. For example, you give $50,000 to ABC Insurance Co. today; ABC promises to pay you $400 a month, starting tomorrow and continuing for the rest of your life.

How are these payments taxed? There's a complicated formula, depending on your life expectancy and prevailing interest rates. Fortunately, ABC (or any other insurance company) will make the calculations and report to you as well as the IRS. If you receive $400 a month, $4,800 a year, perhaps $2,000 a year will be considered taxable income. If you're in a 35 percent tax bracket, you'd owe only $700 in tax (35 percent times $2,000).

If only $2,000 is taxable, what is the other $2,800 you receive? The IRS considers that a tax-free return of your own capital. Naturally, if you live for another 18 years, and get back all $50,000 of your capital, then all the remaining annuity payments will be fully taxable.

TERM LIMITS

Most of the annuities promoted as "tax shelters" really aren't annuities, as just described. Instead, they're *deferred annuities*, which are different. Here, you give money to some other party (often, but not always, an insurance company) and promise to keep your hands off for many years. In return for that promise, the IRS agrees not to tax your investment income.

Some deferred annuities are *single-premium*. You buy them with one large payment, perhaps $25,000 or $50,000. Other deferred annuities call for you to pay in smaller sums, over a period of years. In either case, your account builds up, with no current income tax, until you withdraw your money.

The shelter is in the tax deferral. Here's an example from the American Funds Group of mutual funds:

You invest in mutual funds	$ 50,000
Over 20 years, the annual growth rate is	10%
After paying tax each year, at 31 percent, you'd have	$196,000

Certainly, nothing to complain about. But, according to American Funds, here's what would happen in a deferred annuity instead:

You invest in a deferred annuity $ 50,000
Over 20 years, the annual growth rate is 10%
With no current tax to pay, your account would grow to $360,000

Of course, this is not an apples-to-apples comparison, as American Funds points out. With $360,000 in the annuity account, you'd owe tax on $310,000 worth of gains. If you took all the money out at once, you'd owe about $96,000 in income tax (assuming the same 31 percent rate) and have $264,000, after-tax. Obviously, $264,000 is better than $196,000.

In a more likely scenario, you'd use your $360,000 to purchase an immediate annuity, as described here. Now, you might receive around $3,000 a month, or $36,000 a year—a handsome return on your original $50,000 outlay. Most of that $36,000 would be taxable, but a small portion would be considered a tax-free return of your $50,000 investment.

IN A FIX

You may wonder why the American Funds Group of mutual funds is advocating deferred annuities. That's because American Funds, like many mutual fund "families," sells *variable annuities*. In turn, variable annuities are one type of deferred annuity, as opposed to *fixed annuities*.

Again, "fixed annuities" is a misnomer. Here, you get a fixed rate of return on the money you invest, but that rate is fixed for only a short time. If you're 50 years old, buying a deferred annuity you plan to cash in 15 years later for retirement income, then it's not really meaningful that the insurance company "fixes" the investment return at 7 percent for one year, or even two years. What's going to happen for the next 13 or 14 years? The insurer might drop the fixed rate to 4 percent or 5 percent after the initial period.

Some fixed annuities offer complicated bail-out clauses: If the renewal rate drops more than a certain amount, you can get your money back. But an insurance company determined to play "bait-and-switch" can always get around a bail-out clause.

If you're interested in buying a fixed annuity, insist on seeing the company's history of renewal rates for the past several years, just as you'd insist on evaluating the insurer's financial strength. The *Retirement Income Guide,* published by A. M. Best, Oldwick, New Jersey, lists annuity contracts and shows the history of renewal rates. Call 908/439-2200 for information.

MUTUAL ADMIRATION

An honest fixed annuity will keep paying at a rate comparable to that of high-quality bonds. In 1993, as mentioned, fixed annuity rates were averaging around 7 percent, about what you could earn on a top-rated, medium-term corporate bond. If you see an annuity advertising a surprisingly high rate, you should be doubtful the insurance company will be able to sustain it for any time period.

But what if you're not satisfied with bond-type buildup in your deferred annuity? If you want higher returns, and you're willing to take some risks, consider variable annuities.

Here, you direct how your annuity premiums will be invested. If you choose well, your annuity account will grow rapidly. If you don't, your account may shrink. (There is, however, a guarantee that your beneficiaries will receive at least the amount you contributed if you die while holding a variable annuity.)

Most variable annuities give you a broad choice of investments: stock funds, bond funds, a money market fund. Often, the funds available are managed by the same people who handle big-name mutual funds. Within a variable annuity, you can switch your money around when you want to, although there are certain limits.

Therefore, investing in a variable annuity is like investing in mutual funds without paying taxes right away. Mutual fund investors owe tax on all dividends and capital gain distributions—even if dividends are reinvested, which is the case for 70 percent of mutual fund shareholders. When you switch from one fund to another, you'll owe income tax if you have a paper profit on the first fund.

Inside a variable annuity, all of those taxes are deferred until you take money out. (Variable life insurance policies are similar to variable annuities in that they offer you a chance to invest in mutual funds while avoiding current taxation. Typically, the fees on variable life policies are higher than variable annuity fees. However, for the extra fees you get life insurance protection as well as life insurance tax benefits: tax-free policy loans and income tax-free death benefits.)

Deferred annuities have yet one more tax advantage. If you're unhappy with the one you have, you can exchange it for another without paying tax on the investment income you've already enjoyed. (As a practical matter, the company offering the annuity to which you're switching will help you with the paperwork.)

PAY AS YOU LEAVE

So deferred annuities have their advantages. You can invest your money as you please, in a fixed or variable annuity, and defer the taxes, often for many years. In effect, you can choose when you want to pay tax on investment income. But there are drawbacks as well as benefits to buying deferred annuities.

The toughest hurdle to clear is illiquidity. Once you put your money in, it's expensive to pull it out. Deferred annuities aren't for you if you think you'll need your premium dollars back in a few years. They're strictly long-term commitments.

Under a 1982 change in the tax code, all the money you take out of a deferred annuity gets LIFO (last-in, first-out) tax treatment. For example:

You bought a deferred annuity for	$50,000
After a few years, your account has grown to	$65,000
You have to withdraw	$25,000

All of your investment income ($15,000) is fully-taxed

The rest of your withdrawal ($10,000) is a tax-free return of your own money

Under the old rules, withdrawals were on a FIFO (first-in, first-out) basis, so you could withdraw up to $50,000 as tax-free return of capital. Certain older annuities still qualify for FIFO treatment.

The tax bite is even greater if you make withdrawals before you reach age 59-1/2. On all annuities purchased since 1982, a 10 percent penalty tax applies.

If you have a taxable withdrawal of	$15,000
And your tax bracket is	35%
You'll owe income tax of	$ 5,250
Plus a nondeductible 10% penalty tax of	$ 1,500

Altogether, 45 percent of your withdrawal would be taxable, leaving you with just 55 percent ($8,250 on a $15,000 withdrawal).

In addition, many deferred annuities impose their own surrender charges if you take money out. These surrender charges vary enormously from contract to contract, but one might read: You can take out up to 10 percent of your account each year. In excess of that, you'll pay a 10 percent charge the first year, 9 percent the second year, and so on, until the charge "disappears" after 10 years.

Besides illiquidity, there are other drawbacks to deferred annuities. One is expense: You pay the insurance company or whoever else acts as the sponsor. Again, expenses vary, but you probably pay around 1 percent to 2 percent a year to put your money into a deferred annuity, versus what you would pay to hold money in other vehicles such as CDs, Treasury bonds, or no-load mutual funds.

In addition to incurring expense, you lose some flexibility when you invest in a deferred annuity. With a fixed annuity, you're at the mercy of the insurance company, which sets renewal rates. With a variable annuity, not only do you have investment risk, you have a limited choice of mutual funds.

THE RIGHT STUFF

So when does a deferred annuity make sense? When you meet these criteria:

1. You need to be someone who pays a hefty tax each year on investment income from CDs, mutual funds, stocks, bonds, and the like. If you're not paying a lot of tax, why bother to shelter it?

2. You must be in a high tax bracket. If your bracket is only 15 percent, you're better off paying the tax each year and doing what you want with your after-tax dollars.

3. You must be able to live with illiquidity for several years. The longer you let your money compound, the greater the value of the tax-deferred buildup. Don't buy a deferred annuity unless you're confident you can outlast the age 59-1/2 tax penalty and any surrender charges called for in the contract.

Investors in their late forties to early fifties are often considered ideal prospects for deferred annuities. They're far enough from retirement to benefit from tax-free compounding, yet they're close enough to age 59-1/2 to clear the penalty tax hurdle.

Moreover, investors who are already older than age 59-1/2 may want to buy deferred annuities. Illiquidity isn't as much of a problem because the penalty tax won't apply. If you select an annuity with generous surrender charges, you can put money in and take it out almost at will. In effect, you can invest for income or growth, depending on your preference, and decide when to pay the income tax—when you take money out of the annuity contract.

DIFFERENT STROKES

If you meet the aforementioned criteria, how can you decide which deferred annuity is for you? Conservative investors will want fixed annuities, because your account can go in only one direction—up. Be sure to choose an insurer that's highly rated by Moody's or Standard & Poor's, with a record of setting reasonable renewal rates.

More aggressive investors will prefer variable annuities, with their potential for higher returns. A good portion, if not all, of your premium should go into stock funds—that's where you'll find the greatest potential return. If you're willing to settle for bondlike returns, you're better off in a fixed annuity. So pick a variable annuity that offers stock funds managed by top pros with impressive track records.

SPLIT THE DIFFERENCE

If you're looking for a tax-sheltered way to beat CDs, consider a strategy called "split annuity" investing. Nina Gray, for example, has $100,000 she's been rolling over into CDs. When CD rates are 4 percent, she'll wind up with less than 3 percent a year, after tax.

Instead of investing $100,000 in a CD, Nina puts $50,000 into a deferred annuity and $50,000 into an immediate annuity. Assuming interest rates average 7 percent or 7.5 percent, her $50,000 deferred annuity will grow to $100,000 in about 10 years—that's the equivalent of getting her money back from a CD.

At the same time, Nina chooses a 10-year payout on the immediate annuity. By shopping around, she finds one that pays $7,000 per year, a 7 percent return on her $100,000.

If Nina receives $70,000 from her immediate annuity, over 10 years, $50,000 will be a tax-free return of her principal. On the $7,000 she receives each year, only $2,000 will be taxable. Thus, Nina winds up with after-tax income that's more than twice as much as she'd receive from a CD.

Nina invests $100,000 in a CD paying interest of	4%
Annual interest is	$4,000
In a 30 percent bracket, income tax is	$1,200
After-tax income is	$2,800
On her $100,000, her after-tax yield is	2.8%

Nina invests $50,000 in a 10-year immediate annuity paying annual income of	$7,000
Of each year's income, taxable amount is	$2,000
In a 30% bracket, income tax is	$ 600
After-tax income is ($7,000 - $600)	$6,400
On her $100,000, her after-tax yield is	6.4%

The 10-year period illustrated here is not a rule. You can choose any term you'd like and buy an immediate annuity to match.

Is there a catch? Split annuities lack the federal insurance protection of a CD, but you can minimize the risk by buying from a well-rated insurance company. More seriously, the $100,000 Nina winds up with in her deferred annuity, after 10 years, is not the same as $100,000 in a CD. Of the $100,000 in the annuity account, $15,000 (her $50,000 untaxed gain times 30 percent) is owed the IRS. So Nina really has $85,000 of her own in the annuity account.

In effect, Nina has enjoyed $3,600 per year in extra income (a total of $36,000) while incurring a $15,000 deferred-tax obligation. That's a good tradeoff, considering that Nina can continue to defer the tax until she withdraws money from the deferred annuity.

There is a potential tax trap, too. According to some advisers, the IRS frowns on split annuities if they're sold as a package. The tax-free buildup of the deferred annuity might be challenged. Just to play it safe, buy the deferred and the immediate annuity at different times, from different insurance companies.

In fact, that makes good sense, aside from tax consequences. The insurer with the best fixed annuity (good history of renewal rates) might not be the insurer with the best immediate annuity (high yield for the payout period you want). So shop around on both sides of the split.

LIFE SUPPORT

There's another variation on this strategy. As you remember from the chapter on life insurance shelters, policies that don't meet the seven-pay test are modified endowment contracts. If you buy a MEC, you're not eligible for tax-free policy loans.

Suppose, in the preceding example, Nina is concerned about her son Paul, who's just starting college. If Nina dies, Paul will have to struggle to complete his education.

So Nina sets up the split annuity, as described earlier. She'll receive $6,400 each year, after tax. She decides to keep half for herself, to spend or reinvest. That $3,200 is more than she'd net with a CD.

The other $3,200 per year goes into a cash value policy on her life, projected to have the policy vanish after 10 years. Because she'll be making 10 equal premium payments, the policy passes the seven-pay test and qualifies for tax-free loans. Depending on her age and health, she might buy a $100,000 life insurance policy.

What has Nina accomplished? She has her entire $100,000 working for her, at relatively high interest rates. Except for the $600 she pays in tax each year, on the immediate annuity, all the investment income is tax-free. She provides for her own retirement (through the deferred annuity) and protects her son's ability to pay for his education (with the insurance policy). Plus, she can access the policy's cash value via tax-free loans in case of an emergency. Just to make sure this strategy is completely auditproof, Nina buys the immediate annuity and the insurance policy from different insurers at different times, after shopping the market carefully.

SUMMING UP

- An immediate annuity is a pure annuity, offering you a stream of income in return for a lump sum.
- Deferred annuities offer tax shelter. You pay a premium or premiums and enjoy tax-free buildup until you withdraw your money.
- Fixed annuities pay bondlike yields that are reset periodically.
- Variable annuities offer you a choice among investment vehicles, including stock funds and bond funds.
- The drawbacks to deferred annuities are expenses and illiquidity.
- The best prospects for deferred annuities are investors who won't need to cash out before they reach age 59-1/2.
- Split annuities offer a way to more than double the after-tax income you'd earn on CDs.

8 Happy Endings
How to Take Money Out of a Deferred Annuity

Whether you invest in a fixed or a variable deferred annuity, the time will come to take out your money. If you keep all your money in the buildup stage, until your death, you'll leave your family with a huge tax bill. All the deferred income tax will be due.

For example, suppose you bought a deferred annuity for $100,000. Over the years, tax-free compounding enables your investment to increase to $300,000. At your death, your untaxed $200,000 gain will be immediately taxed. Moreover, the annuity value will be included in your taxable estate; if your estate is large enough (see Chapter 22), the annuity will be subject to estate tax as well, taxed around 50 percent.

Therefore a deferred annuity really is a deferral—you save tax now and pay tax in the future, when you take your money out. The longer the deferral, the more valuable the tax shelter, but you can't wait too long or you'll stick your survivors. In most cases, the time to begin taking money out is when you retire. Then your annuity can supplement Social Security, other retirement plans, and so on. (Unlike IRAs, Keoghs, and so forth, you don't have to begin annuity withdrawals at age 70-1/2. Typically, you can defer withdrawals until age 85, if you want. But that's not a good idea if you're concerned about estate tax.)

OPTIONS PLAYS

You'll have to decide how to take money out of a deferred annuity. Typically, the insurance company (or any other financial institution providing a deferred annuity) will recommend that you "annuitize" your contract. However, that's not always the best way.

When you annuitize, you enter into a new contract, one that calls for a stream of payments. In most cases, the annuity stream will be for the rest of your life, thus providing you with income you'll never outlive.

In the last chapter, a basic annuity was called an immediate annuity. When you annuitize, you're converting your deferred (that is, buildup) annuity to an immediate (payout) annuity.

Say Joe Thomas invested $25,000 in a deferred annuity from Great American Life Insurance Co. when he was 50 years old. Now that he's 65 and ready to retire, his $25,000 has grown to $100,000. If he annuitizes, he's purchasing an immediate annuity for his $100,000.

When Joe approaches his insurance company, he'll likely be offered a bewildering array of annuity options, including:

- *Single-life annuity.* This is the simplest, easiest to understand, choice. Joe gives the insurance company his $100,000 in return for the promise of a lifetime income. The insurance company will look at Joe's age (not his health), the current interest-rate environment, its forecasts for investment returns, and quote Joe a number. Great American Life might offer $800 a month, $1,000 a month, $1,200 a month, or whatever. Those payments will continue as long (or as short) as Joe lives.

  A single-life annuity is a crapshoot. Suppose the monthly payment is $1,000. Joe could have a heart attack and die three months later, after receiving $3,000 in payments. If so, that's it. The insurer gets to keep all the rest of Joe's money.

  On the other hand, Joe might live to be 99 years old: 34 more years, 408 more months. In that case, the insurer will pay $408,000 to Joe, quite a windfall on the $100,000 he annuitized.

Because of the risks involved, the payments on a single-life annuity will be higher than for any other type of lifetime annuity.

- *Joint-and-survivor.* A single-life annuity, with its rich payout, may be suitable for individuals with no dependents. As long as there's no one else to worry about, you might as well get the greatest income possible.

However, Joe does not want to choose a single-life annuity because that jeopardizes his wife, Kate, age 60. If he dies, say, in five years, a single-life annuity will expire, while Kate, then 65, would face the rest of her life with a reduced income.

Therefore, a joint-and-survivor annuity keeps paying as long as either Joe or Kate is alive; they both have the security of a lifetime income. In this case, though, Great American Life has much more risk. Not only are two lives covered, but one is a 60-year-old female; Kate could easily live another 20 or 25 years. Therefore, the monthly payout on a joint-and-survivor annuity will be much lower than a single-life payout. In fact, the joint-and-survivor annuity might be the lowest of all the lifetime options.

If a single-life annuity pays a monthly income of	$1,000
A joint-and-survivor annuity might pay monthly income of	$ 700

Now, instead of $12,000 a year, Joe and Kate receive only $8,400 a year, a sizable difference.

Joint-and-survivor annuities needn't cover a married couple. Joe might, for example, cover himself and his son, John, who is 40. Because John is so young and his life expectancy so long, the monthly payout will be much lower.

- *Period certain annuities.* As a compromise between the high risks of a single-life annuity and the low payout of a joint-and-survivor annuity, "period certain" annuities are popular. In fact, a

10-year period certain might be the most common choice among annuitants.

Here, you're buying a single-life annuity, but with a guaranteed minimum payout. Thus, period-certain annuities tend to have a payout in between single-life and joint-and-survivor annuities.

If a single-life annuity pays a monthly income of	$1,000
A joint-and-survivor annuity might pay monthly income of	$ 700
A 10-year period-certain annuity might pay monthly income of	$ 850

Now, if Joe lives until age 99, he'll still collect all that time, but the total will be around $350,000 instead of over $400,000. If he dies after three months, though, the insurance company is obligated to keep paying until a total of 120 payments (10 years' worth) are made. Thus, 117 additional payments would go to Kate, or any other beneficiary named by Joe.

Altogether, then, the insurance company will pay out at least $102,000, over 10 years. That's not a great return on $100,000, but at least Kate has some protection. In the meantime, they'll keep receiving $850 a month if Joe lives beyond the 10-year period. So they have upside (a chance to receive hundreds of thousands in annuity payments) without any chance of actually losing their money.

There are other annuity payout options, but they're basically variations of the ones already described.

DRAWING OUT THE DEFERRAL

If Joe annuitizes his contract, he gets yet another tax break. Under the tax code, he can spread out (that is, defer) his already-deferred tax obligation.

Say he takes the $850 a month, 10-year period-certain option. The insurance company will calculate how much of each payout is taxable and how much is a tax-free return of his $25,000 investment.

For example, he might get a $104 return-of-capital and $746 worth of taxable income. Here's the result if Joe's retirement tax bracket is 30 percent:

Monthly annuity income is	$850
Taxable portion is	$704
Tax obligation @ 30% is (704 x .30)	$211.20

Thus, Joe pays roughly 25 percent of each annuity payment in tax, keeping 75 percent. This continues for 240 payments (Joe's 20-year life expectancy), until all of Joe's $25,000 capital has been returned, for tax purposes. Subsequent payments are fully taxed. (For annuities purchased before 1987, the shelter continues indefinitely.) If you're older when you annuitize, and the portion of investment earnings in your account is smaller, you'll get more tax shelter with each monthly payment.

TIES THAT BIND

Although the tax consequences of annuitization are favorable, other aspects are not. People in poor health, for example, will come out losers if they fail to reach their life expectancy.

In addition, there's a natural temptation to stay with your original issuer. Joe, for example, simply stopped after getting quotes from Great American Life. However, there usually are huge differences in the amounts offered by different insurers, even on different contracts. First National Life, for example, might make a much higher offer on a joint-and-survivor policy while International Life might quote a higher figure for 10-year certain. So Joe is much better off if he shops around before annuitizing. There are no tax consequences for switching from one insurer to another.

A greater drawback to annuitizing is the lack of flexibility. Joe locks himself in to receiving $850 a month for the rest of his life. If inflation spikes up in a few years, that $850 won't buy what it used to. Even with moderate inflation, that $850 a month will lose half of its value over 15 to 20 years.

Some insurers offer a "variable" payout option, similar to a "variable" buildup. Here, Joe can choose how he wants his $100,000 to be invested, among stock funds or bond funds or money market funds. Instead of a fixed dollar amount, he might receive 1 percent per month or 0.5 percent a month or some other percentage. Thus, if the account value continues to increase because of excellent investment results, his monthly payout can increase, too, keeping up with inflation.

Variable payouts, though, haven't caught on. Most retirees naturally are reluctant to take risks with their income—payouts can drop if results are poor. Plus, variable payouts usually start lower than fixed payouts. Some insurers are working on innovative variable payout methods, which might make them more attractive, but variable payout alternatives are used rarely, as of this writing.

GET POOR QUICK

Losing flexibility is something you may be able to live with; losing wealth is quite another matter. Yet that is exactly what happens whenever you annuitize a deferred annuity.

Consider Joe Thomas, in the preceding example. One moment, he has an annuity account with a $100,000 valuation; the next moment he has nothing more than $850 a month in income.

Suppose Joe has an emergency and needs some cash. Or he'd like to help one of his children make a down payment on a house. As long as he has a $100,000 account value, he can get at his money. Once he annuitizes, he loses that nest egg. (Some insurers permit annuitants to borrow against a period-certain annuity, but that's not always the case.)

So what's the alternative? Some advisers tell investors to keep the money in the buildup stage, even during retirement. You can take money out, as needed, by making withdrawals. In this way, you can take out large or small amounts, to suit your needs. You have flexibility, access to all of your money, and the money not withdrawn continues to compound, tax-free. If, for example, Joe removes $8,000 a year and the account earns 8 percent, his balance will remain around $100,000. As he grows older, and the future tax bite on his heirs becomes more of a threat, he could take out larger amounts, drawing down the account.

This strategy would be ideal...except for taxes. Under the 1982 tax law, all deferred annuities purchased since then are taxed on a LIFO basis, as mentioned. Withdrawals are taxable until you've taken out all the investment income. Then withdrawals are tax-free returns of your principal.

Joe Thomas, for example, invested $25,000 in an annuity that's now worth $100,000. The first $75,000 worth of withdrawals are fully taxable. Only after Joe gets down to his original $25,000 will withdrawals be tax-free.

This sounds like a sizable disadvantage: If Joe annuitizes, he gets 20 years' worth of partially taxed withdrawals, but if he just makes partial withdrawals, they'll be fully taxable until he strips his account down to $25,000. In practice, though, the difference isn't all that great. As explained earlier:

If Joe annuitizes and receives monthly income of	$850.00
His net after-tax income is ($850 - $211.20)	$638.80

Suppose Joe decides not to annuitize but takes partial withdrawals instead:

If he makes monthly withdrawals of	$850
He'll owe income tax @ 30 percent of (850 x .30)	$255
His net after-tax income is	$595

Thus, by paying extra tax of $43.80 a month, about $525 a year, Joe retains full access to his $100,000 account.

If he increases his withdrawal to $900 a month, he'll net about $630 a month, nearly the same as he'd net with a monthly annuity of $850. If he withdraws $900 a month, that's $10,800 a year, or 10.8 percent of his original portfolio. Assuming Joe can earn 8 percent or 9 percent on the balance, the annuity value will drop by only a couple of thousand dollars a year. He'll be able to maintain such withdrawals for at least 15 years, maybe 20, depending on his investment success. All the while, he maintains his flexibility and the ability to annuitize when he wants to.

So what's the best way to take money out of an annuity? You're probably best served by making modest withdrawals at first, to see how much you really need. While you're doing so, you can shop around, looking for the best annuity deal. And you can have the insurer's actuaries crunch some numbers for you, figuring in your age, your amount invested, and your account value, to see how much tax you'd owe if you annuitized. Once you have some hard numbers, you can compare annuitizing versus withdrawals, side by side. Don't jump to annuitize until you have all the facts in front of you.

THE OUTLOOK

How solid are the tax advantages of annuities? In the 1990s, proposals have surfaced to do away with tax-free compounding under certain circumstances. These proposals haven't gone anywhere because relatively little revenue would be raised and a social purpose—encouraging people to save for retirement—would be set back.

Nevertheless, some of the tax shelter of deferred annuities might be scaled down. If so, the changes likely would be prospective rather than retroactive. That's what happened when the tax laws on annuity distributions were tightened in 1982. So if you invest in a deferred annuity before any tax revisions are approved, you likely will lock in the tax breaks.

SUMMING UP

- With a deferred annuity, the deferred income taxes must be paid sometime, during your lifetime or at your death.
- One way to get your money is to annuitize, which entitles you to a stream of monthly payments.
- A single-life annuity provides high income but puts your loved ones at risk.

- A joint-and-survivor annuity can provide lifetime income for yourself and your spouse but the payout rate is low.
- A popular compromise is the period-certain annuity, which is a single-life annuity with a guarantee of a minimum number of payments.
- Annuitizing locks you into a fixed income and robs you of access to principal.
- Therefore, you might want to pay slightly more in taxes and tap your account via partial withdrawals instead.

9 Cut the IRS out of Your Investments

More Ways to Pay Lower Taxes on Investment Income

The words "limited partnership" don't exactly stir warm feelings in the hearts and minds of investors. In the 1980s, billions of dollars were invested in limited partnerships—and billions of dollars were lost. Some limited partnerships turned out to be good deals, even very good deals, and others may yet prove to be decent. But most investment LPs failed to provide the promised returns.

So limited partnerships aren't at the top of the list of audit-proof tax shelters. Not only were they bad investments, in many cases, some turned out to be lousy tax shelters: The IRS disallowed deductions and slapped investors with penalties in addition to interest.

Nevertheless, limited partnerships can provide some tax shelter. Some LPs are clean, from a tax point of view, with a chance of being good investments as well. To learn how to mine the few nuggets, you need to keep an open mind on LPs.

In essence, a limited partnership is a form of doing business, a cross between a regular (that is, "general") partnership and a corporation. With a general partnership, the partners share the profits or losses, according to their agreement. However, all partners are liable for any debt incurred by the partnership.

A corporation, on the other hand, provides liability protection for shareholders. If you invest in Exxon, for example, and Exxon is hit by a huge damages award, no one will come after you to pay your share.

But corporations suffer tax disadvantages. There's the corporate income tax to pay. Then, all dividends are fully taxed if you're an individual shareholder. The only way to avoid this tax is to hold shares within a sheltered retirement plan.

PASSING THROUGH

Enter the limited partnership, an alternative business structure. The general partner runs the business and assumes all the liability. The limited partners, like corporate shareholders, have limited liability. However, they're still partners, for tax purposes. If the partnership has a loss, it's passed through to the limited partners.

Originally, limited partnerships were made up of small groups, often people who knew one another. Then limited partnerships became sold as packaged investments. In the 1970s and early 1980s, so-called "private placements" were heavily peddled to wealthy investors. Often, these deals required large investments and offered huge tax benefits. Tax abuses, when they occurred, tended to be in this type of LP.

The next stage of LP evolution was the "public program," immensely popular in the mid-1980s. As the name suggests, they were sold to just about everyone. They usually required small investments, perhaps $5,000. Promised tax benefits were modest, but there was little audit risk.

The limited partnership game fell apart in the late 1980s. First oil prices collapsed, damaging oil and gas LPs. Then the 1986 tax act removed the ability to deduct LP losses, in most cases. Real estate LPs crumbled as the real estate market tumbled. Finally, the 1990–1991 recession damaged various other LPs in equipment leasing, cable TV, and so on. All in all, not a great experience for most investors.

RUBIES IN THE RUBBLE

Still, a few deals held up. The problem was not in the LP structure, but in the underlying businesses. While real estate, oil and gas, and other LPs were sinking, for example, several marine cargo-container LPs were paying over 20 percent a year to investors, thanks to the boom in world trade that ran from the mid-1980s well into the 1990s.

As of this writing, not many newly formed partnerships are being offered for sale to investors. There are a few, though, that offer the chance for tax-sheltered income without any meaningful audit risk.

- *Real estate*. Some new LPs own fast-food restaurants, which are leased to franchisees. The franchisees promise to cover all expenses plus the lease payment to the LP. Judging by past performance, successful LPs of this nature will distribute about 8 percent a year. On a $10,000 investment, you might receive $800.

  Moreover, the LP may be taking deductions for mortgage interest, depreciation, and other expenses. Those deductions are effectively passed through to you, as a limited partner, so maybe you'd report only $500 worth of income to the IRS. The other $300 is sheltered. (In truth, you'll eventually pay the tax when the properties are sold, but you may be able to enjoy a favorable capital gains rate.)

  Because limited partnerships are in such disrepute these days, and because of added paperwork, some real estate fund raisers sell their deals as real estate investment trusts (REITs) rather than limited partnerships. The principle is the same, and some REITs generate tax-sheltered cash flow.

- *Oil and gas*. Another type of LP buys properties where oil and gas have been discovered. The oil and gas is produced and sold, over a period of years, and the proceeds divided among the limited partners. Here, the depletion allowance (a deduction similar to depreciation) is passed through to investors. On a $10,000 investment, you might receive $1,000 in cash yet recognize only $500 in taxable income. Again, some of the cash flow is sheltered.

The catch here is that you're literally getting your own money back with each barrel of oil that's sold. At some point, perhaps years in the future, production will run out and you'll stop getting checks from the LP. Then, that's it. There's no building to sell, to get some or all of your money back. When you received that $1,000 a year, it was $500 in income and a $500 return of your own capital.

- *Leasing.* These partnerships buy anything from computers to airplanes to cargo containers. The equipment is leased and the lease payments passed through to investors. Payouts can be very high, 15 percent or more a year. That cash flow will be partially sheltered, maybe even fully sheltered, because depreciation deductions are usually sizable.

  Unfortunately, leasing deals "turn around." After the equipment is fully depreciated (which may take only a few years), there's no shelter left. Then, all of your cash flow likely will be fully taxable; you may even wind up owing more tax than the cash you receive, if the LP is repaying loans. And your final payoff is uncertain, depending on how valuable your equipment is at the end of the line. A marine container may be extremely valuable, if there is a strong worldwide demand, but how much can you expect to get for a 10-year-old computer?

STRICTLY BUSINESS

Other types of investment partnerships may be offered, but the basic premise is the same. If the deal is successful, you can earn substantial income, sheltered by depreciation or depletion deductions. Except for some specialized partnerships (see Chapter 11), the tax benefits available now are not overwhelming. To make an LP worthwhile, the underlying business has to succeed. For example, if oil and gas prices shoot up, the aforementioned oil and gas partnerships likely will do well.

As mentioned, oil prices sagged in 1985. If you had invested in the PaineWebber/Geodyne Resources Income Fund 1-D then, you would have cashed in on the subsequent surge in oil prices, receiving all of your money back, in distributions, by the end of 1991, with cash continuing to flow as of this writing.

Don't put too much of your money into LPs. However, you might want to put a few dollars into out-of-favor industries, such as real estate. Just be sure you read over all the materials first, so you can tell where your money will be going. If you invest well, you can earn substantial cash flow, fully or partially tax-sheltered.

MASTER PLANS

Some limited partnerships are called master limited partnerships (MLPs) or publicly traded partnerships (PTPs). They're businesses organized as LPs rather than as corporations, and they trade like stocks, on an exchange or over-the-counter. Perhaps the best-known PTP is the Boston Celtics pro basketball team. Others include Cedar Fair, which runs amusement parks, and EQK Green Acres, which operates a large shopping center on Long Island, near New York City.

Because these PTPs owe no corporate income tax, distributions can be significant. At the beginning of 1993, when the average S&P 500 stock was paying a dividend under 3 percent, the Celtics were paying over 7 percent, Cedar Fair over 6 percent, and EQK Green Acres over 12 percent. What's more, all of those PTP distributions were partially sheltered by a pass-through of tax deductions.

SECOND TIME AROUND

There's yet another way to find shelter in limited partnerships. By the early 1990s, offerings of new LPs were rare. After past disasters, there weren't many willing investors, so few new deals were brought out.

However, there are hundreds of partnerships left over from the 1980s, with thousands of investors. Many of those investors want to sell their shares, called partnership "units." If you know what you're doing, you may be able to buy partnership units at an excellent price on an informal "secondary market" established by brokerage firms.

For example, the PaineWebber oil and gas fund described earlier originally sold units for $1,000. In 1992, when it was distributing around $200 per unit per year, units traded on the secondary market as low as $280 apiece. Or, take the IEA Marine Container Income Fund IV, which was distributing $110 per $500 unit (22 percent) in 1992. On the secondary market, units sold for as low as $360 that year, generating a current yield of over 30 percent.

So there are chances to make money in LPs and to receive that money partially tax-sheltered. Ask your broker for information on the LP secondary market or call Liquidity Fund, the largest participant, at 800/227-4688. But you have to treat these LPs the same way you'd treat the stocks of emerging companies with extremely small market capitalizations: with a lot of caution.

NOT JUST FOR BABIES

At the other end of the spectrum from limited partnerships is perhaps the safest, even stodgiest, tax shelter of all: EE Savings Bonds.

EE bonds are issues of the U.S. Treasury, so they enjoy the same tax advantage of all Treasury obligations: the interest is exempt from state and local income taxes. Suppose you're a New York City resident who invests in Treasury bills. The interest income you receive will be subject to federal income tax but it will escape New York State and New York City income taxes. The same is true if you invest in Treasury notes or Treasury bonds. That's why investors in high-tax areas love Treasuries. EE bonds offer that same tax exemption.

With EE bonds, though, there are extra tax advantages. You can, if you wish, defer the federal income tax bite, perhaps for many years. Suppose you buy a $100 EE bond for $50. Over the years, the value of the bond will increase, to $75, $100, $150, and so forth. No tax will be due until you cash the bond in, which can be delayed for up to 30 years.

On the other hand, you can choose to recognize the interest every year. If the bond is held by a child, perhaps, with very little other income, recognizing the income each year can result in little or no tax.

TAX-FREE SAVINGS BONDS

As of 1990, there's another possible tax advantage to EE bonds. For bonds bought in that year or later, income tax can be avoided altogether if the proceeds are used to pay for a child's tuition and educational fees. This tax break, however, applies only if you're at least 24 years old when you buy the bond and your taxable income when the bonds are redeemed is less than about $75,000, on a joint return ($50,000 on a single return). If your income is higher, you'll get a partial tax exemption, which disappears as your income reaches about $105,000 (joint) or $80,000 (single). (The income levels go up each year, with inflation.)

In addition to all these tax advantages, EE bonds are surprisingly decent investments. In 1993, for example, they paid a solid 4 percent, higher than the yield on money market funds. What's more, EE bonds are indexed, so the yield will go up if inflation accelerates.

You have to hold onto EE bonds for at least five years to get the guaranteed yield and the benefit of indexing. If you held on for only six months, however, the yield was 2 percent in early 1993, nearly as much as you could have earned on six-month CDs, which are fully taxable. So EE bonds make sense for the most conservative investors seeking tax shelter.

ONCE IS ENOUGH

In between low-risk EE bonds and high-risk limited partnerships is the great middle ground that appeals to most investors: mutual funds. As mentioned earlier, you can shelter taxes on mutual funds by investing through tax-deferred retirement plans, variable annuities, or variable life insurance policies. If you invest in mutual funds

directly, you'll owe taxes on all distributions (even if they're reinvested) and all profitable sales. When you move money out of a
fund—even if it's to another mutual fund—it's considered a sale by
the IRS. The same if you take advantage of a mutual fund's
checkwriting privilege. If your shares have gone up in value, you'll
owe tax.

However, many mutual fund investors pay more tax than they
need to. If you can legally trim that tax obligation, the net effect is
the same as finding an audit-proof tax shelter.

For example, most mutual fund investors automatically reinvest dividends. In turn, these investors often pay too much because
they forget to add these dividends to their "basis" (cost for tax
purposes).

Suppose Sandy Larkin invested $1,000 in ABC Mutual Fund
several years ago. Since then, she has reinvested $230 worth of
dividends. Now, with her ABC shares worth $2,000, she is switching
from ABC to XYZ Mutual Fund.

Sandy reports a $1,000 capital gain to the IRS—she bought at
$1,000 and sold at $2,000. However, her true basis is $1,230: the $1,000
she paid plus the $230 in reinvested dividends. She already has paid
tax on those dividends so there's no need to pay tax again. Therefore,
she has only a $770 taxable gain.

Note that most of that $770 is a long-term capital gain, taxable
at no more than 28 percent. Only the shares bought with dividends
within a year of sale are short-term gains, exposed to regular income
tax rates.

PARTIAL PROBLEMS

If Sandy wants to sell part of her ABC shares, figuring the tax is
trickier. She can, if she wants, calculate an average price-per-share.
Suppose, at the time of sale, she owns 190 shares of ABC. Because
her basis is $1,230, as calculated here, her average price per share is
$6.47. Selling at $10.50 per share, she reports a taxable gain of $4.03
for each share she sells.

Another method is the "first-in, first-out" method. Here, if Sandy sells 100 shares she would add up the costs of the first 100 shares of ABC that she bought and use that as her basis. However, if ABC has appreciated over the years, this method will increase her tax bill.

She's much better off if she can specify which shares she wants to sell. Suppose ABC is selling at $10.50 per share and she wants to raise $1,000. Sandy would have to sell about 95 shares. Going over her records, she could see which 95 shares had the highest cost and instruct the fund to sell those. (For example, "Sell the 10 shares bought July 10, 1992,...."). Selling the highest-cost shares will give you the smallest taxable gain. Naturally, you need to keep complete records to be able to do this.

Fortunately, a growing number of mutual fund families are sending shareholders "tax-cost statements," which include the date, price, and dollar amount of each purchase or sale. These statements also show the average price per share. American Capital, Colonial, IDS, Keystone, Oppenheimer, Pioneer, and Putnam are among the families that prepare these statements, with others sure to join the trend; Keystone and Pioneer are particularly cooperative in allowing you to specify which shares will be sold.

SUMMING UP

- Although limited partnerships have disappointed many investors, they can pay distributions that are partially sheltered from income tax.
- When investing in an LP, focus on the underlying business. If it's successful, the tax benefits will enhance your return.
- Shrewd investors willing to take risks may find good buys on the LP secondary market.
- EE Savings Bonds offer excellent tax advantages, including deferral, exemption from state and local income tax, and possibly exemption from all tax if they're used for education expenses.

- Besides safety and tax benefits, EE bonds are surprisingly good investments in a low-interest rate environment.
- Many investors overpay tax on mutual fund investments. Avoiding excess tax payments is as effective as finding a tax shelter.
- To avoid paying excess taxes on mutual fund transactions, keep careful records and specify shares whenever you sell.

10 Real Shelters

Cut Your Taxes by Buying Investment Property

During the late 1970s and early 1980s, a breed of investment known as "tax shelters" enjoyed a population explosion. These deals ranged from real estate and oil drilling to cattle breeding and lithographs. The premise, though, was basically the same.

Investors would put up some cash; the deal, in turn, was structured to generate tax deductions or tax credits or both. Altogether, the tax savings were expected to be more than the cash invested. You invested $10,000, for example, and cut your taxes by $15,000. Thus, you were $5,000 ahead.

A series of tax laws passed in the 1980s dimmed the appeal of these tax shelters and finally eliminated them. Almost. There still are investments you can make that will actually cut your tax bill. Before explaining them, however, some tax-code clarification is necessary.

THE THREE Ps OF PAYING TAXES

There are now three kinds of "income"—think of them as paycheck, portfolio, and passive income. Paycheck income is the simplest to understand. If you get compensated for work you've done, that's paycheck income (otherwise known as ordinary income).

Portfolio income generally comes from conventional savings and investment vehicles. If you have dividends from stocks or mutual funds, interest from bank accounts or bonds, then you have portfolio income.

Passive income, the third category, is a bit trickier. In general, passive income is income from a business in which you don't actively participate. Rental real estate is considered a passive activity, by definition, so income from real estate is passive. Similarly, income from a limited partnership is passive.

Under this classification, most of the old tax-shelter deals were categorized as passive activities. Income, if any, is passive income; losses are passive losses. Shelters generally aimed to provide "paper" losses through accounting gimmicks.

Suppose Larry Jackson bought a limited partnership interest in a lizard ranch back in 1983. The ranch still reports annual tax losses, passing a share through to Larry. Under the tax code, those losses are passive losses.

That's the problem. Passive losses can't be used to offset ordinary or portfolio income. Larry can't use his lizard ranch losses to offset his regular income as a rock musician or his interest and dividend income. Passive losses can't reduce capital gains, either.

If Larry has passive income—perhaps from a profitable real estate venture—he can use the lizard ranch passive loss as an offset. Most people, though, don't have passive income. Without passive income, passive losses can't be deducted, usually until the deal winds up and the losses are real losses. That's why the old-style tax shelter deals are virtually extinct now: They may still produce losses but investors won't be able to deduct those losses. (Tax credits generated by passive activities are treated the same way. They can reduce the tax on passive income but not on other types of income.)

EXCEPTIONAL OPPORTUNITY

There are still a few exceptions to the passive-loss rule. For most people, the prime exception is rental real estate. If you own rental property and take a tax loss, you probably can deduct that loss against your regular income, perhaps up to $25,000 a year. Just as important, rental real estate can be a lifelong source of tax-free cash.

Let's say Jill Jackson was smarter than her brother, passing up the lizard ranch deal. She kept her money in stocks and bonds, took her profits in 1991, and bought into the depressed real estate market. She acquired a shopping center that was in foreclosure, paying $100,000 down and borrowing $900,000 to buy a $1 million shopping center.

As the economy recovered, Jill's shopping center prospered, generating a $90,000 profit in 1993. That is, the total of the rents Jill received exceeded all of the operating expenses, insurance, property taxes, and so forth, that she paid. In real estate lingo, that $90,000 was her net operating income (NOI).

As mentioned, Jill borrowed $900,000 to buy her center. Assume she has a 9 percent, interest-only mortgage, so she pays $81,000 a year. That still leaves her with $9,000 a year in "positive cash flow," as the real estate people put it.

Annual rental income	$ 300,000
(Minus) all operating expenses	$–210,000
Net operating income	$ 90,000
(Minus) mortgage interest ($900,000 x 9%)	$ –81,000
Cash flow	$ 9,000

So Jill has a 9 percent cash return on her $100,000 outlay, cash-on-cash. However, when she fills out her tax return, she doesn't report $9,000 in taxable income. That's because she's entitled to a deduction for depreciation on the property.

As a rule of thumb, real estate depreciation is about 3 percent a year. On a $1 million shopping center, that's $30,000 in annual depreciation. So when Jill files her tax return, the depreciation deduction turns her $9,000 gain into a $21,000 loss.

That's a passive loss, which Jill couldn't usually deduct. However, the tax code has a special provision that will allow her to deduct that $21,000 loss.

GAIN BY LOSING

Assume Jill is in a 35 percent tax bracket (federal and state). A $21,000 loss saves her $7,350 in taxes. Now her total return from the venture is $16,350: $9,000 in untaxed cash flow and $7,350 in tax savings. That's a 16.35 percent return, after tax, on her $100,000 investment.

As you can see, the tax shelter here has almost doubled the investment return. In order to qualify for the shelter—that is, in order to be able to deduct the loss—several criteria must be met:

- You must own at least 10 percent of the property.
- You can't own your share as a limited partner.
- You must play an active role in property management.

That doesn't mean you have to patch the ceiling and replace the washers. You don't even have to manage the property day by day; it's all right to hire a property manager and a rental agent.

However, you do have to play a role in important decisions. Should rents be raised? How much of a capital improvements budget is necessary for this year? Not only should you participate in these decisions, it's important that you keep a record demonstrating your input.

As a practical matter, it's easier to support a claim that you're an active manager if you live or work near the property, so you can make frequent site visits. If you live in Michigan, say, and rent out a condo in Florida, you should make at least a few trips to your property each year, meeting with the management firm, to justify your claim.

THE $25,000 QUESTION

Finally, there are restrictions on the amount of real estate losses you can deduct. The basic rule is that you're entitled to deduct up to $25,000 worth of losses a year. However, if your adjusted gross income (AGI) is over $100,000, your ability to use passive losses from investment real estate declines.

If your AGI is over $150,000, you can't use any such losses to offset other types of income. (As mentioned, passive losses can offset passive income.) Between $100,000 and $150,000 in AGI, your available loss drops by $1,000 for every $2,000 in AGI.

In our example, Jill has a $21,000 passive loss. She can take a full deduction as long as her AGI is under $108,000. If her AGI is over $108,000 she can deduct some or none of her $21,000 loss.

Jill's AGI is	$108,000
Excess over $100,000	$ 8,000
Divide excess by 2	$ 4,000
Subtract from $25,000 passive loss allowance	$ 21,000

Thus, with an AGI of $108,000, Jill is entitled to deduct up to $21,000 in losses from actively managed real estate.

If her AGI were $125,000, her deduction would be limited to $12,500. The other $8,500 loss, that she can't deduct, has to be carried forward to another year in which she will be eligible for the deduction.

HOLDING PATTERN

There's yet another catch to this shelter. The $30,000 depreciation deduction that Jill takes is not a present from the IRS. Every time she takes a depreciation deduction, she reduces her "cost basis" in the property.

Say, for example, that she holds onto the shopping center for three years, taking $90,000 in depreciation deductions, dropping her basis from $1 million to $910,000. Then she sells it for $1 million.

Jill thinks she's broken even—bought for $1 million, sold for $1 million. The IRS, though, sees that her basis was $910,000 and the selling price was $1 million. Jill has a $90,000 taxable gain: She has to pay tax on all the depreciation deductions she has already taken.

In the real world, Jill will be reluctant to sell the property and pay this tax. Instead, she'll hold on as long as possible, hoping for appreciation.

Suppose, for example, Jill holds the shopping center for 10 years, at which point NOI has increased from $90,000 to $150,000 a year. The center is appraised at $1.6 million. Jill goes to the bank and refinances, taking out a $1.3 million mortgage. She pays off the old $900,000 loan and puts the remaining $400,000 in her pocket, tax-free.

Not bad for a $100,000 investment, especially since Jill has enjoyed 10 years of tax-free cash flow and tax savings.

TRADING PLACES

Ten more years pass and Jill is ready to retire and move to Arizona. What will she do with her old shopping center in Minnesota? Her basis now has fallen to $400,000 and the property is valued at $2.2 million. If she sells for that $2.2 million, she'll have a $1.8 million taxable gain and owe the IRS hundreds of thousands of dollars.

There is yet another audit-proof tax shelter she can use. It's called a tax-free exchange. In essence, you can exchange one piece of investment property for another without owing any taxes. (You can't use tax-free exchanges for personal residences.)

Here's Jill with a shopping center in Minnesota she no longer wants. Once she retires and moves to Arizona, she won't be able to keep an eye on her Minnesota property. She'd much prefer to own real estate in Arizona.

Therefore, Jill goes to Arizona on an inspection visit. She finds a retirement community where she'd like to live. Then, she tours the surrounding neighborhood, eventually finding a nearby apartment building where the owner is willing to sell. After looking over the property, it seems to her that the value of the Arizona apartment building is about the same as her Minnesota shopping center.

(Note that a tax-free exchange doesn't have to involve a shopping center for a shopping center or an apartment building for an apartment building. Any type of investment property can be exchanged.)

STEP BY STEP

Now, it certainly would be too much to expect that the owner of the Arizona apartment house is willing to exchange his property for a shopping center in Minnesota. Such exchanges are possible, but that's not usually the case.

Instead, Jill can bring in a third party, an intermediary or an "accommodator." The contract between Jill and the accommodator will state that this is one step in a planned exchange.

Jill will sell her shopping center to a local buyer. The proceeds, however, go to the accommodator, instead of to Jill. Then the accommodator uses the money to buy the shopping center in Arizona, on Jill's behalf. (If Jill holds the money from the first sale, the IRS won't consider the transaction a tax-free exchange.)

The result: Jill has a property in Arizona instead of Minnesota. No taxes are due. Now Jill can retire to Arizona and keep an eye on her property there. If she has chosen well, she'll receive rental income from the property, or she'll be able to refinance it and take out some tax-free cash.

Jill hopes to hold onto her property until she dies. Under current law, her heirs will inherit and get a "step-up in basis" to market value, avoiding all the capital gains. That is, if she dies while the property is worth $3 million, her heirs could sell the property for $3 million and all the prior appreciation will be untaxed.

(There have been proposals to tax appreciation at death or to carry over Jill's basis to her heirs. In practice, such changes in the tax law would create a tremendous amount of complexity for little gain in revenue, so Congress has backed away.)

EXCHANGES RATE

Does this shelter work? Definitely. The IRS lost a key court decision in the Starker case, which upheld a deferred, three-way exchange. Then Congress passed a law that specifically permits such exchanges. In some sections of the United States, exchanges are more common than outright sales of real estate.

Nevertheless, you need to work with a savvy real estate lawyer who'll be able to follow all the rules. Under the tax code, within 45 days of selling your original property, you must specify which properties you'll use as a replacement. You can name several properties. Then you'll have another 135 days to purchase a replacement property, finishing the exchange.

In some cases, exchanges work the other way. You might buy the replacement property first, then seek a buyer for your old property. Unfortunately, you have neither case law nor tax law on your side when claiming this is a tax-free exchange. Experts differ on whether these deals really avoid taxes. To play it safe, try to sell your old property before you buy a new one.

Moreover, you'll seldom find a property that's exactly equal in value to the one you already own. Typically, one property is worth more than the other, which means some cash must be included to "balance the equities." Therefore, you'll probably have to come up with some cash, called "boot," or you'll owe tax on the cash you receive. Plus, you'll owe money to the attorneys and accommodators involved.

Still, if you're holding a property with a sizable untaxed capital gain, you'll find it well worth your while to go through the formalities of a tax-deferred exchange.

CRAWL BEFORE YOU WALK

All these examples of tax advantages may make real estate investing seem easy. It's not. In most cases, you have to look hard to find the right property at the right price. Then you need to manage the property for years to cash in on long-term appreciation.

So don't rush into investment real estate, even if the $25,000 allowable tax deduction looks appealing. If you've never been a real estate investor, start small. Buy a single-family house or a condo to rent out. If you're buying a more expensive property, line up a partner or two to share the burdens with you.

Look for a property with a history of tenant rentals, so you can see how much rent you're likely to receive and how high expenses are likely to run. Buy only if the projected income exceeds projected expenses. Crunch some numbers to see if you'll still have positive cash flow, even after paying mortgage interest.

Borrow as much as you can but not so much that the mortgage payments exceed income from the property. Try for "nonrecourse" debt; that is, if you default on the mortgage, the borrower can seize the property but not come after your personal assets.

Buying right is the key to successful real estate investing. Once you have real estate profits, there are ways to get at your paper profits, tax free, and avoid paying tax on your gains.

SUMMING UP

- Most investments sold as tax shelters generate passive losses, which can't be used to offset ordinary or investment income.
- An exception to the passive-loss rule is actively managed real estate.
- If your adjusted gross income is under $150,000, you may be able to deduct up to $25,000 in losses each year from investment property you actively manage.
- Rather than sell investment property and pay tax on capital gains, you may receive tax-free cash by refinancing.
- Tax-free exchanges of investment property can extend the tax benefits.
- Under current law, tax obligations for asset appreciation are wiped out at death, so it pays to hold appreciated investment property until you die.

11 Where Credit Is Due

Real Estate Tax Credits to Shrink Your Tax Bill

Besides the deduction for actively managed investment properties, described in the previous chapter, there are two other real estate tax shelters you can use to offset your ordinary income. Both shelters offer tax credits, which reduce your tax bill, dollar for dollar. That is, a $1,000 tax credit can reduce your income tax obligation from, say, $5,000 to $4,000.

One type of tax credit, perhaps the simplest to use, is available if you fix up an old building. Fix-up costs on buildings placed in service before 1936 can generate 10 percent tax credits. To qualify, you must spend at least as much on rehab as you paid to buy the property, and you can't gut the building.

For example, Greg Harmon buys a small downtown office building, dating back to the 1920s, for $100,000 and spends $300,000 on rehab costs. He's entitled to a $30,000 tax credit—10 percent of $300,000.

HISTORY LESSONS

There's even more tax shelter available if you rehab a building that's "historic" or located in a historic district. For such buildings, the tax

111

credit is 20 percent. Historic buildings or districts are certified by local preservation agencies.

To claim this credit, you must use investment property rather than a personal residence. And there is an extensive procedure you must go through to get your rehabilitation approved, so you can claim the credit. Your local preservation agency likely can help you with the paperwork.

In essence, you'll get approval only if your rehab will preserve the building's appearance, especially the facade. That's why preservation societies are so eager to help in many cases. An old building can be brought into the twenty-first century without destroying the look of the neighborhood.

You might, for example, take a little-used manufacturing building and convert it to an urban shopping mall. An old bakery might become a suite of professional offices. By restoring the original architectural features, you may attract tenants and even enhance the value of your property.

UNPLEASANT SURPRISES

There are risks, though. For one, you never know until work actually is underway how much it will cost to install modern electricity and plumbing and air-conditioning in a turn-of-the-century building. Cost overruns may be unavoidable.

In addition, a rehabilitated building—especially a historic rehab—is really a new building. Past financial statements mean little. You won't know until you're finished how much rent you'll be able to collect from tenants attracted by your combination of elegant appointments and modern conveniences.

So approach rehabs with care. You should have some experience with real estate renovation or work with someone who has. And be sure to keep careful records. The more you can show to have spent on the rehab, which includes planning, the more tax credits you'll be able to claim.

ONE-TWO PUNCH

You can parlay real estate tax shelters here. Assume Milt Black buys an old hotel in his city's downtown historic district and converts it to an apartment building. He spends $200,000 to buy the building and $600,000 on rehab. After all the paperwork is finished, he's entitled to a $120,000 tax credit (20 percent times $600,000).

He can take this $120,000 tax credit even if he spent only $80,000 of his own cash, borrowing the other $720,000.

Once the apartment building is up and running, Milt is entitled to the tax breaks mentioned in the previous chapter. He can claim depreciation, a noncash deduction. As long as he actively manages the property, he can deduct up to $25,000 a year in losses if his adjusted gross income is under $100,000 and smaller losses if his AGI falls between $100,000 and $150,000.

There are, however, limits on the 10 percent and the 20 percent rehab tax credit. Because this credit is considered "passive" (it doesn't matter if you drive in every nail yourself), you're restricted on how much ordinary income it can shelter. In most cases, you can use a $25,000 "deduction equivalent."

In other words, you can take a credit that would save you as much tax as a $25,000 deduction. Say you're in the 28 percent tax bracket. A $25,000 deduction would cut your tax obligation by $7,000 (28 percent times $25,000). Thus, you're entitled to a rehab credit of up to $7,000 a year.

If you're in the 31 percent tax bracket, you can use a $7,750 credit. In a 36 percent tax bracket, you could use up to $9,000 worth of rehab credits.

That's still not the end of the complication. Assume you file a joint return with $105,000 in taxable income in 1994, and the 31 percent tax bracket kicks in at $95,000. Your $25,000 deduction equivalent would consist of $10,000 at 31 percent and $15,000 at 28 percent, for a total of $7,300 maximum credit you can take. If you earn more credits than the maximum you're allowed, you can carry the excess to future years.

HITTING THE CEILING

Suppose you have both rehab credits and actively managed real estate losses in the same year, either from different properties or the same one. You can't use more shelter than a $25,000 deduction equivalent.

Phyllis Evans is solidly in the 28 percent tax bracket for 1993, so her $25,000 deduction equivalent will save her $7,000 in taxes. If she deducts $6,000 from an office building she owns ands actively manages, that leaves her with a $19,000 deduction equivalent left. So she can take an additional $5,320 in rehab tax credits. Altogether, the credit and the deduction can cut her tax bill by $7,000.

This assumes that Phyllis has no taxable passive income, perhaps from yet another real estate venture. If she does, she could offset all the passive income with passive losses and passive tax credits, then offset another $25,000 worth of ordinary income.

There's a further complication for anyone whose AGI is over $200,000. As explained, such investors can't deduct losses on actively managed real estate (because of AGI over $150,000), but they can take rehab credits. Once your AGI goes over $200,000, your ability to use rehab credits begins to phase out, $1 per $2 of AGI, until it disappears at $250,000. With $210,000 of AGI, for example, you could use up to $20,000 worth of deduction equivalents, in rehab credits, against ordinary income.

So much for tax simplification. When you consider a real estate rehab investment, crunch some numbers with your CPA. That's especially true if you're mixing rehab credits with losses from actively managed real estate. Moreover, look beyond the rehab tax credit to the final project. You won't make money from the tax credit alone, but the rehab credit can reduce your startup costs and thus make it easier for you to earn a profit (and all the tax advantages) from investment real estate.

NOT JUST FOR DO-IT-YOURSELFERS

Rehab tax credits can be a do-it-yourself tax shelter, but there are other ways to earn them. You might, for example, combine with some friends to form a partnership. In this way, you'll share the costs and the responsibilities.

In the preceding example, Milt Black might form a partnership with four other people he knows. Instead of an $80,000 investment, he'd put in only $16,000, assuming equal shares. And he'd have four people to help him do the rehab and qualify for the tax credit.

The $120,000 tax credit, then, would be awarded to the partnership. Each of the five partners would claim a share—a $24,000 tax credit—on his or her individual tax return.

Taking this one step further, you can buy into a widely sold limited partnership, available through many brokerage firms. Often, you can invest as little as $5,000 to become a limited partner, with no further responsibilities or obligations.

The general partner (the manager of the partnership) might rehab one property or several properties, passing through your share of the credit. On a $10,000 investment, you might get a $1,000 or a $2,000 or a $3,000 tax credit, depending on the structure of the deal. Then, you'd share in any cash flow or any profits generated by the real estate.

Investing in a limited partnership is easier than doing it yourself, but you lose control over your own money. So make sure the general partner has some experience in rehabbing old buildings and turning them into profitable real estate properties.

THE BIG EASEMENT

There's another tax shelter connected to rehab tax credits, but it's by no means audit-proof. In fact, the IRS focuses on this particular tax break, so you have to proceed super-carefully if you decide to claim it.

First, you (or the general partner of your limited partnership) promises that your building's facade will never change. This is a formal promise, in writing, to a local preservation society. Most important, this promise is binding on all future owners.

Bill Peters rehabs an old stable, converting it into a garage. He promises never to change the facade of the stable-garage. When

Susan Thomas comes along, 20 years later, to turn the garage into a fast-food restaurant, she must retain the original facade.

Thus, there's a loss of value when you make this sort of "easement donation." Bill's garage would have more resale value if subsequent owners didn't have to retain the facade.

To implement the tax deduction, Bill gets before-and-after appraisals to determine the loss of value from the easement donation. The difference is considered a charitable deduction, immediately deductible. As a charitable deduction, it's not subject to the passive-loss rules.

The IRS frequently claims that such deductions overstate the actual loss of value. If you attempt to claim an easement deduction, always use an independent appraiser with an impeccable reputation. And beware of limited partnerships that state an intent to claim this deduction—an IRS challenge may mean an audit for each investor.

DO WELL WHILE DOING GOOD

Besides rehabilitation, the other type of real estate tax credit covers low-income housing, which has become an enormously successful tax shelter. And no wonder. With a low-income housing deal, you actually can make money on the tax benefits alone. What's more, this is a tax shelter you can point to with pride because you're helping the less fortunate to enjoy decent housing. (This shelter has become so important that *The New York Times* ran a headline in February 1993 lamenting, "Delay in Renewal of Low-Income Housing Tax Credit Threatens Projects.")

Low-income housing tax shelters have been around since there have been federal low-income housing programs. Going back to the 1960s, these shelters generally have delivered what they promised to investors, with little protest from the IRS. Such deals offer tax benefits rather than cash flow or capital gains, so they weren't wrecked by the real estate slump of the late 1980s.

Before 1986, low-income housing was a "writeoff" shelter. Investors used relatively small down payments and huge mortgages to finance low-rent housing for tenants. Interest and depreciation deductions were sizable, leading to tax losses.

You might invest	$10,000
In a deal that generated a tax loss of	$30,000
In a 50% tax bracket, that loss would cut your tax by (50 percent x $30,000)	$15,000
So you'd be ahead by ($15,000 tax savings - $10,000 investment)	$ 5,000

As you can see, a wealthy individual might invest $50,000 or $100,000 and cut his tax bill by $75,000 or $150,000. A few provisions scattered around the tax code helped to make low-income housing a desirable shelter. However, low-income housing shelters were generally the creation of accountants and tax attorneys, who cobbled together various tax wrinkles to make the deals work.

The rules changed with passage of the 1986 tax act. Since then, you can find tax shelter in low-income housing with the explicit backing of the federal government.

Passive losses were no longer deductible, as explained. So, in the preceding example, you'd have a $10,000 investment and no tax saving.

Congress could have gotten around this by exempting low-income housing from the passive loss rules. However, the 1986 tax law also reduced tax rates. Take the aforementioned example and plug in a 28 percent tax bracket. A $30,000 loss, even if fully deductible, would save you only $8,400 in taxes. Why invest $10,000 to cut your taxes by $8,400?

SURER SHELTER

To keep low-income housing alive as a tax shelter, the 1986 law created a new tax break. For the first time, Washington specifically spelled out the rules for using low-income housing as a tax shelter. Follow them carefully and you'll get your tax savings without worrying about the IRS.

The new low-income housing shelter substitutes tax credits for tax deductions. Investors who qualify for the low-income housing tax credit will receive these credits for 10 consecutive years.

In the real world, the rules are complicated enough so you probably don't want to buy an apartment and rent to low-income tenants. Instead, real estate firms raise money through public limited partnerships, generally with a $5,000 minimum for investors.

The partnerships raise millions of dollars with which they buy dozens of apartment properties across the country, tend to the paperwork necessary to qualify for government subsidies, and make sure the apartments are rented to low-income tenants. Often, many of these apartments are rented to the elderly. Otherwise, the tenants are workers earning below the local median. The apartments aren't urban housing projects with welfare tenants; frequently, low-income housing partnerships buy properties in small towns or rural areas, where wear and tear on the buildings won't be severe.

CREDIT, NOT CASH

The partnerships receive the tax credits and pass them through to each partner, pro rata. Investors generally receive around 15 percent per year in tax credits.

If you invest	$10,000
You can expect to receive annual tax credits (@ 15%)	$ 1,500
Over 10 years, you'll save	$15,000

Not only will you be ahead by $5,000, that will be $5,000, after-tax. You'd have to earn about $7,500 in interest, and pay around $2,500 in income tax, to wind up with an equivalent return.

There's a tradeoff you have to make in return for the tax credit. You're not likely to receive much cash flow from rents. Tenants usually pay no more than 30 percent of their income. A retiree living on $450 a month from Social Security might be paying $135 a month to rent an apartment that otherwise would be renting for $400 or $500 a month. The rental income goes almost entirely to debt service, operating expenses, and property maintenance, without much left over to distribute to investors. (On the bright side, with rents so low the apartments are sure to be nearly 100 percent rented.)

Although the credits run for 10 years, it may actually be 12 years before they're all used, because of startup lags on some properties. Then what? The law says that the apartments must be maintained as affordable housing for an additional five years.

After that, in many cases, the properties can go to market rents. Practically speaking, that's not likely to happen. No government, federal or state or local, is going to want to see a retiree evicted from a $135-a-month rental so a rock star can move in and pay $500 a month. Every effort, no doubt, will be made to keep these properties affordable, long after the 15- to 17-year period is up.

GUESSING GAME

But who will operate and maintain a property with perpetually low rents and no chance of a profit? In many states, there's a year-long period before the restrictions phase out, during which housing authorities can find a "suitable buyer," such as a nonprofit housing group.

Another alternative, perhaps the most likely, is to find another group of investors who'll be able to start the tax credit cycle all over again. The problem with this solution, neat as it seems, is that no one knows whether the tax credit or anything like it will still be in existence in 2008 or 2009, and so forth.

Investors need to be concerned about what will happen then. If there's a buyer—a nonprofit organization or a new tax shelter partnership—for the properties tomorrow, today's investors stand to get their money back, in addition to all the tax credits. You'll wind up with an effective return equal to around 15 percent per year, after-tax.

However, if there's no buyer at the end of the line, today's investors may simply walk away from the properties rather than paying to maintain them. In that case, you'll get a tax loss in addition to the tax credits. If your $10,000 investment is a total loss, you'll save $3,000 to $4,000 in taxes, in addition to the roughly $15,000 in tax credits you've received.

LIMITED LARGESS

These deals are so firmly in the "too good to be true" class that there's a limit to the use of the low-income housing credit. Again, you can use a "deduction equivalent" of $25,000 per year, just as with rehab credits. In the 31 percent tax bracket, for example, you can use up to $7,750 per year.

A 31 percent bracket effectively places a $52,000 cap on investments in low-income housing partnerships. If the credit is 15 percent, that's $7,800 per year, right at the $7,750 limit.

You invest	$52,000
You receive in annual tax credits about ($52,000 x 15%)	$ 7,800

As you might suspect, the tax credit comes with a laundry list of wherefores and whereases. This credit can't be used in years when you're subject to the alternative minimum tax (AMT). If you use other real estate tax shelters—the rehab credit or the deduction for active management of rental property—that will trim your allowable low-income housing credit. Altogether, you can get the equivalent of a $25,000 tax deduction per year. (More if you have passive income to shelter.)

You own a rental property that generates a tax loss of	$10,000
Your "deduction equivalent" is now ($25,000 - $10,000)	$15,000
In a 31% bracket, you can still use low-income housing	
credits of (31% x $15,000)	$ 4,650

Suppose you invested $40,000 in a deal and you get a $6,000 credit (15 percent). You can use $4,650, in the previous example, but what happens to the other $1,350? You probably will be able to carry unused credits forward and use them in the future.

On the other hand, suppose you have taxable income from a "passive activity," such as rental property. You can use excess low-income housing tax credits to offset the tax you owe from these ventures. So check with your tax preparer before investing in low-income housing.

IN FOR THE LONG HAUL

What if you invest in this shelter and you need cash five years from now? You can sell your partnership shares, or "units," if necessary, before the partnership winds up, as long as there are still tax credits to be realized. However, new investors will want a discount so you should plan on holding for 15 years or so.

If you're ready for a long-term commitment, be sure to invest with a proven sponsor. There are so many things that can happen in that time period, so many technical requirements to comply with, you want to be assured your sponsor will deliver the desired tax credits, year after year. Many brokers sell low-income housing partnerships, but don't buy until you've seen evidence of a sponsor's past performance.

Free research reports on some low-income housing partnerships are available from Standard & Poor's Real Estate Financial Group, 26 Broadway, New York, NY 10004. For information on specific sponsors' past performance, call Robert A. Stanger & Co., Shrewsbury, NJ, at 900/786-9600; the cost is $5 per minute.

POPULAR APPEAL

As of this writing, the low-income housing tax credit is not a permanent part of the tax code. Instead, the credit comes up for renewal each year. Some investors are afraid they'll lose their credits if the tax break is not renewed, but that's not the case. The renewal relates to future projects. Once the tax break has been cleared for a given year, the money is allocated for 10 years of tax credits. So investors who qualify for the credit in 1994 will get 10 years' worth of credits, even if the tax law changes in 1995.

Actually, there is little likelihood the tax credit will be abandoned. In late 1991, when the credit was renewed, the vote was 420–0 in the House, 100–0 in the Senate! In 1993, when President Clinton proposed higher taxes on wealthy Americans, he specifically asked for a renewal of the low-income tax credit. The tax credit now accounts for most federally subsidized low-income housing and is perhaps Washington's favorite tax shelter.

SUMMING UP

- A tax credit reduces your tax obligation, dollar for dollar.
- There is a 10 percent tax credit for money spent on rehabbing buildings placed in service before 1936.
- Historic rehabs qualify for a 20 percent tax credit.
- Rehab tax credits help cut your start-up costs but you still need a profitable real estate venture to come out ahead.
- The most practical way to benefit from low-income housing tax credits is to invest in a large, publicly sold partnership.
- Such partnerships buy apartments and rent them to low-income retirees and workers, not to no-income welfare recipients.
- Investors receive tax credits equal to about 15 percent of their investment, each year, for 10 years.
- Altogether, you'll get a positive return from the tax benefits alone and an excellent return if you get your money back from sales of the apartments.
- For many people, investments in such partnerships are limited to $52,000, which will cut your taxes by about $7,800 per year.
- If you take advantage of other real estate tax shelters, your ability to use the low-income housing and the rehab credit will be reduced.
- Always check out the experience and reputation of the sponsor before investing in a low-income housing shelter.

12 Last of the Write-off Deals
Drilling for Shelter in Oil and Gas

The old packaged tax shelters are gone, killed by the passive loss rules. There is, though, one type of tax shelter you can still buy into for an unlimited, legitimate write-off: drilling for oil and natural gas. When the 1986 tax act was passed, industry lobbyists (representing independent producers, not necessarily the name-brand oil companies) succeeded in keeping this tax break.

Drilling shelters depend on one specific tax break, established long ago and still in the tax code. That's the deduction for intangible drilling costs, or IDC.

In the case of most new businesses, start-up costs are largely capitalized or amortized: They can be deducted only over a period of years. Thanks to the IDC deduction, though, most start-up costs involved in drilling for oil and gas can be deducted right away.

Let's say, for example, that the Lane sisters, Linda, Lois, and Lucille, form a partnership at the end of 1994 to drill for oil. They spend a total of $100,000. Their accountant looks over their records and tells them that $90,000 qualifies for the IDC deduction.

Naturally, it takes a while to drill the wells, bring up the oil and gas that's discovered, and sell the finished products. So the 1994 results for the Lane Sisters Partnership look like this:

Gross Revenues	0
Deductible Expenses	$90,000
Net Loss	($90,000)

Because each sister has an equal share in the partnership, each can report a $30,000 loss for this venture for the year.

Normally, such losses would be considered passive losses and probably would not be deductible. Thanks to an exception carved out in the 1986 tax act, however, investors can deduct these losses, as long as they don't invest as limited partners or use some other technique to limit their financial liability. Therefore, each Lane sister can use this up-front loss to reduce her 1994 income and her tax obligation.

That may be fine for the Lane sisters, who grew up in Oklahoma and know their way around a drilling rig. How can less knowledge-able investors use this tax shelter?

You can, if you want, invest in a partnership sold through a brokerage firm. The minimum investment typically is $5,000. Such shelters are usually sold late in the year so the first income will be deferred into the next year. Depending on the deal, you might get a 50 percent to 90 percent write-off. For each $5,000 you invest, you might deduct $2,500 to $4,500. Usually, you get the deduction in the year you invest.

DEDUCT NOW, PAY LATER

Some deals, usually aimed at wealthy investors who'll contribute larger amounts, may offer even more tax shelter. Suppose Joe Rich agrees to put $50,000 into a drilling deal, expecting a 90 percent ($45,000 write-off). He may be able to pay in $10,000 a year for 5 years. In the first year, then, he might make a $10,000 cash outlay and still get a full $45,000 write-off, saving him $18,000 in taxes that year, in a 40 percent tax bracket. He's $8,000 ahead of the game.

What's more, oil and gas drilling can be a last-minute shelter. Joe Rich can invest his $10,000 in November 1994, or even in early December, and still get a $45,000 write-off on his 1994 return, as long as the wells are started by March 1995 and there's a genuine reason (such as fixing his costs) for the prepayment.

In the following years, if the venture strikes oil or gas, Joe will share in any sales proceeds. What's more, the "depletion" allowance may reduce his tax on that income. If Joe receives $10,000 in 1995, for example, the depletion allowance may shelter $2,500, so he'd pay tax on only $7,500 worth of income.

In a drilling shelter, investors can use "percentage depletion," a particularly valuable tax break. Percentage depletion continues as long as the well produces income. Joe may wind up sheltering more income than he actually invests.

Some oil and gas investors use another tax angle. Joe might wait until he's claimed the IDC deduction in the first year or two. Then he can give away his interest to his teenaged daughter, Carla, who's in a low bracket. Subsequently, all the income flows to Carla, sheltered by the depletion allowance. If all goes well, Carla can build up a sizable college fund.

COVER YOUR ASSETS

However, Joe can't get the deduction if he invests as a limited partner. He must invest as a general partner in a partnership or as a joint-venture investor. This puts his assets on the line in case of a drilling accident, say, or an environmental disaster.

To reduce such risk, sponsors of these deals commonly carry liability insurance; they may agree to put their own assets in the path of creditors, before investors' assets. A common strategy is for Joe to invest as a general partner, then convert to a limited partner after the drilling deductions have all been taken. The IRS has said this is okay.

Practically speaking, investors in these deals haven't been hit with huge liability claims. They have, though, suffered generally miserable returns over the years. Often, too much of the money has gone into the sponsor's pocket rather than into the ground. And the prices of the oil and gas—especially the natural gas—have been depressed, lowering the returns to investors.

Drilling for oil and gas sounds like risky business. The problem with many of these deals is that they're not risky enough. After the money is raised, drilling is done in areas where oil and gas already have been discovered. This is called "developmental drilling," and there's not much chance of hitting a dry hole. If oil has been found half a mile north of your well and half a mile south of your well, chances are that your well, too, will strike oil.

But developmental drilling often is disappointing. "Decline curves" are steep, meaning that production tapers off quickly after an initial encouraging "flush." After five years, your well may be producing little or nothing, giving you little or no return.

THE CASH MUST FLOW

This tendency of developmental wells to peter out is discouraging because you need a stream of oil and gas revenues for a successful investment. If you invest $5,000 and get a $4,500 write-off, you'd save $1,800 that year, in a 40 percent bracket. You'd still have $3,200 at stake ($5,000 minus your $1,800 tax savings). Without $3,200 in oil and gas revenues, you've lost on the deal.

Or consider Joe Rich, who invested $10,000 the first year and saved $18,000 in taxes. He has to make four more payments, $10,000 apiece. Unless he earns a substantial amount from the drilling fund, he'll have to go into his own pocket for the deferred payments, losing money on the venture.

Therefore, don't go into a drilling program because it's a tax shelter. Invest only if you want to be in the oil and gas business—you expect prices to rise, for example. Check carefully on the sponsor's record, to be sure he or she has actually been involved in some deals where investors have gotten back more money than they've put in.

AVOIDING THE AMT

Unlike the real estate shelters mentioned earlier, where deductions are limited to $25,000 per year (or the equivalent in tax credits), drilling shelters have no such ceiling. You can, in theory, write off $50,000 a year, $100,000 a year, or even more,

However, the IDC deduction is considered a "tax preference item" for purposes of calculating the alternative minimum tax (AMT). In some cases, the same is true of percentage depletion. Depending on several factors (your income, the amount of preference items, other tax breaks you use), going into a drilling fund can subject you to the AMT and effectively wipe out your tax shelter.

Before you make a sizable investment in this type of shelter, check with your tax preparer.

SUMMING UP

- Investing in programs that drill for oil or natural gas can generate large write-offs that same year.
- The deductions may be available even if the investment is made late in the year, as long as there's a legitimate reason for a year-end prepayment.
- If your drilling investment is successful, the proceeds may be sheltered by the depletion allowance.
- In order to enjoy up-front write-offs, investors can't use the shield of limited liability, so it's vital that adequate insurance be in place. After the drilling is done, investors may convert to limited partner status.
- A drilling fund's success will depend on oil and gas revenues rather than on tax benefits, so look for a sponsor with a good record.
- Invest cautiously in these shelters so you don't wind up paying the alternative minimum tax.

13 Shelter Begins at Home
Tax Breaks for Homeowners

Tax laws come and tax laws go. Every few years, there's a wave of "tax reform," which washes out certain credits and deductions. Just as ebb tide follows high tide, tax reform is followed by an effort to stimulate the economy with new (sometimes the same) credits and deductions.

One tax shelter, though, is largely immune from tax code trauma. The deduction of mortgage interest may not be as American as Mom or apple pie, but it's not far behind. The congressperson who proposes the abolition of this deduction is a representative who's already planning his or her retirement.

One reason for the deduction's popularity is its simplicity. If you own a home (or a condo or a co-op apartment), and if that home is mortgaged, you can deduct the interest. The same is true if you pay mortgage interest on a second home that you use for weekends and vacations.

Let's say Al and Beth Collins buy a house for $120,000, paying $30,000 down and borrowing $90,000 from a local bank, taking out a 30-year, 10 percent mortgage. Each month, they'll pay around $790 to the bank, or $9,480 a year.

At the end of the year, they'll get a statement from the bank, designating the amount that was paid for interest. In the first year, approximately $9,000 will be interest while the other $480 will be a repayment of the loan principal. Thus, Al and Beth can deduct $9,000 on their tax return. This deduction is itemized on Schedule A of Form 1040.

If they don't itemize deductions, they won't be able to use the write-off. However, most people with home mortgages itemize their deductions. As long as you itemize deductions, you're also entitled to deduct local real estate taxes you pay.

THE RICH GET RICHER

The deduction for home mortgage interest is virtually an inalienable right, unlikely to trigger any IRS interest. However, its value as a tax shelter is limited.

For one thing, the deduction merely limits your cost of housing. Let's say, for example, that Al and Beth are in a 35 percent marginal tax bracket, counting federal, state, and local income taxes. With a $9,000 writeoff, they'll save $3,150.

Deduction reduces taxable income by	$9,000
In a marginal tax bracket of	35%
The tax savings is ($9,000 x 35 %)	$3,150

If Al and Beth have paid $9,480 on their mortgage for the year, the tax shelter reduces their net cost to $6,330. Thus, the main value of this tax break is to make housing more affordable.

Like any other tax deduction, this tax benefit is worth more to those with high incomes. If Al and Beth were in a 15 percent tax bracket (low-to-moderate income, no state or local income tax), their deduction for mortgage interest would save them only $1,350 a year; if they had a large income and a 45 percent tax bracket, they'd save over $4,000 with this deduction.

Mortgage interest deductions dwindle over time. As noted, Al and Beth paid down $480 on their mortgage the first year. Thus, the balance has been reduced from $90,000 to $89,520. The second year, even though they still pay $9,480 a year, the tax deduction is reduced to around $8,950. And so on. Each year, more of your money goes to reducing your loan balance and less to tax-deductible interest pay-ments. By the tenth or fifteenth year of a 30-year mortgage, you're getting much less shelter on your home mortgage.

HIGH RETURNS, NO RISK

Typically, when you buy a house, you stretch for a mortgage. Al and Beth, for example, figured their mortgage would cost them about $6,000 a year, after-tax. At that time, that was about all they thought they could afford.

Ten years later, the after-tax cost of the mortgage is around $7,000, as the interest deduction has been reduced. Meanwhile, Al and Beth have prospered in their careers, so they have more income than before. Now they have money to save and invest. In most cases, you can send extra money to your bank and those funds will be applied to your outstanding mortgage balance. The question is, should they put their discretionary income into prepaying their mortgage?

The answer to this question involves some simple math. When you prepay your mortgage, you're investing at the mortgage interest rate. Because Al and Beth have a 10 percent mortgage, any money they send in for prepayments will earn 10 percent.

That's pretax. Money they prepay will reduce their tax benefits, so their net return on the prepayments will be reduced. To get an after-tax return, multiply the tax rate by the mortgage rate, then subtract that result from the mortgage rate.

The mortgage rate is	10%
Their marginal tax bracket now is	40%
Multiplying the tax bracket by the mortgage rate equals	4%
Subtracting that result (4 percent) from the mortgage rate equals	6%

Thus, prepaying the mortgage will result in a 6 percent after-tax return for Al and Beth. That's a better return than they'd earn from a bank account or a money market fund, where the after-tax return might be around 3 percent. Even if Al and Beth are planning to make long-term investments in the stock market, where the returns have been 10 percent to 12 percent per year, over the past decades, pre-paying the mortgage still looks good. Assuming a 40 percent tax bracket, you'd net 6 percent to 7.2 percent per year. Why take stock market risks when you can earn 6 percent, after-tax, risk-free?

Are there any circumstances when you should not prepay a mortgage? The higher your tax bracket and the lower your mortgage rate, the less it makes sense to prepay your mortgage. If you're in a 45 percent tax bracket, for example, and you have an 8 percent mortgage, prepaying a mortgage will net you only 4.4 percent. You'll probably do better investing in stocks or bonds.

PUTTING YOUR HOUSE ON THE LINE

There's another way to get a home mortgage deduction: Take out a home equity loan. Typically, a home equity loan is a line of credit, which means you don't borrow all the money at once, and you pay interest only on the money you borrow. This line of credit is called a "home equity" loan because it's secured by the equity you have in your house.

Say 15 years have gone by and Al and Beth have paid down their original $90,000 mortgage loan to $85,000. They need some cash (maybe they want to put their kids through college), so they apply for a home equity loan. Their lender sends out an appraiser, who finds that the Collins' house has appreciated in value from its $120,000 purchase price to a current value then of $200,000.

Here's how the lender calculates the Collins' home equity:

Current value	$200,000
Outstanding mortgage debt	85,000
Home equity	$115,000

Each lender will have its own formula for establishing a credit line. Suppose, for example, a lender's limit is 80 percent of home equity. With $115,000 in home equity, 80 percent equals $92,000. So the Collins might get a home equity line of $90,000.

That line might sit there, untouched, for a year or more. Al and Beth owe no interest. Then, to pay for college tuition, they use $20,000 of their line. Now they're paying interest on the $20,000 they've actually borrowed, not the entire $90,000 line.

Where's the tax shelter here? Because a home equity loan is secured by your house, or by a second home, the interest on your loan is tax-deductible. If Al or Beth had taken a personal loan to pay college tuition, or had used credit cards, the interest would not be deductible.

Therefore, home equity loans make sense for almost anyone who has home equity. You can use your credit line whenever you want, for whatever purpose you want. Interest rates tend to be relatively low, and the interest is tax-deductible. (However, the IRS will deny the deduction if you tap a home equity loan to buy tax-exempt bonds or single-premium life insurance.)

Shop around before you take out a home equity loan. Although some banks charge three percentage points over the prime rate, others charge only one percentage point over, or even the prime rate itself.

Also, ask about the pay-back terms. You may be able to use the loan for five years—or for 30 years. Then the pay-back period starts, typically from 10 to 20 years. Some banks offer rollover loans: Wells Fargo in California, for example, has a 12-year loan that can be rolled over for another 12 years.

NOT FOR THE FAINT-HEARTED

If you think there must be a catch to home equity loans, you're right. Most seriously, you're risking your house. In case you can't repay the loan, the lender could force you to sell your house to raise the money.

There are lesser problems, too. Home equity loans often have adjustable interest rates. If rates rise, your monthly payments could shoot up.

Plus, home equity loans taken out after October 13, 1987, have a $100,000 limit. On amounts over $100,000, the interest isn't deductible. Thus, you're better off taking a large mortgage when you buy the house rather than a $100,000+ home equity loan, because first mortgages taken out after October 13, 1987, are fully deductible as long as the total of the new mortgages is $1 million or less.

As is so often the case with the "simplified" tax code, taking out a home equity loan can be even more complicated. The $100,000 limit applies only if your home equity exceeds $100,000. If your home equity (fair market value minus outstanding mortgages) is $75,000, for example, only $75,000 worth of home equity loans qualifies for the interest deduction.

One way to get around the $100,000 limit on home equity loans is to get a second mortgage and use the loan proceeds on home improvements. Such loans are added to your first mortgage and are thus subject to the $1 million limit. However, second mortgage loans often have higher interest rates than home equity loans.

Despite these drawbacks, a home equity loan remains one of the most powerful tax shelters around. In essence, you can borrow what you want and deduct the interest. Like all powerful tools, home equity loans should be used with care.

ALL IN THE FAMILY

Besides using your own house as a shelter, you also can use your child's house. Often, young adults need help in buying a house. If you provide that help, you can find tax benefits as well as a home for your child.

The tax advantages essentially come in two forms. First, there's tax-bracket arbitrage. Say your children are in a 15 percent tax bracket—they'd get little use out of the tax deductions for mortgage interest and property tax. Even if they're in the 28 percent bracket, your tax bracket might be much higher.

In such cases, it pays for you to buy the house and own it, or at least own a portion of it. Then you'd be entitled to the tax write-offs, worth more in your higher tax bracket. Your child would pay full or partial rent to you, as a tenant. Often, the family comes out ahead by shifting deductions to the higher bracket.

In many cases, you can give your child the option to buy the house from you at fair market value. Your child can exercise this option when his tax bracket is high enough to make full use of the tax deductions.

The other tax advantage is depreciation. You also can take write-offs for depreciation if you own all or part of the house, as long as you rent it to your child at a fair market rent. Even if tax brackets are roughly the same, you can benefit from depreciation deductions.

FAIR SHARES

Such shelters are known as shared-equity financing arrangements (SEFAs), and they come in all shapes and forms. Working with a savvy tax pro, you may be able to put together a SEFA that will make the most of the tax shelter.

For a look at a real-life SEFA, take the case of Myra, a California kitchen designer who helped her son and daughter-in-law buy a $256,000 house. Of the required $56,000 down payment, Myra put up $38,000 (68 percent) and the young couple paid $18,000 (32 percent). Because the youngsters agreed to pay the property taxes and most of the mortgage interest, the SEFA arrangement actually calls for them to own 42 percent of the house while Myra owns 58 percent.

The three of them took out a $200,000 mortgage with a monthly payment of $1,640. Because a fair rent for the house is $950 a month, the couple pays Myra $551 (58 percent of $950).

In practice, the young couple pays a total of $1,640 a month—the amount of the mortgage payment. After paying $551 a month to Myra, they send a check to the mortgage lender for $1,089, which they deduct. Myra, who gets $551 a month in rent, sends $551 to the mortgage lender, for a full offset. (This paper chase proves that a fair rent was paid.) In addition, she takes a $4,049 depreciation deduction for her share of the house, saving her $1,134 in taxes each year.

So here's the bottom line. Myra gets what is essentially a 3 percent after-tax return on her down payment, risk-free, through depreciation deductions. When the house is sold, she'll earn 58 percent of any profits. At the same time, she helps her son and daughter-in-law and their two children enjoy a nice home.

THE IRS LOOKS THE OTHER WAY

One more tax shelter is worth mentioning in this chapter. If you have a second home that you use for weekends or vacations, you may rent that house for 14 days or less per year and no tax will be due! You might receive thousands of dollars for renting your beach house in mid-July, yet legally owe not a penny in tax.

SUMMING UP

- On a personal residence or a second home, mortgage interest (up to generous limits) and property tax payments are deductible.
- Prepaying a mortgage can be a low-risk, high-return investment.
- You can deduct interest on home equity loans (secured by your house), up to certain limits.
- Shop around for the best terms on home equity loans.
- You may enjoy tax advantages by buying a house, in full or in part, for your children to live in.
- You can rent a second home for up to 14 days per year without owing any tax.

14 Stacking up Shelters

Trade up in the Housing Market for Lifelong Tax Avoidance

Most people think their house is a tax shelter because mortgage interest and property taxes are deductible, as explained in the previous chapter. Those are tax breaks: The real shelter comes if your house appreciates in value.

This may seem like a fantasy, in the early 1990s. In many parts of the United States, home prices have stayed flat or have even dropped sharply since the late 1980s.

However, the United States has gone through real estate cycles before. If you avoided buying at a market top, and if you hold onto your house for 10 or 15 or 20 years, you likely will see your house go up in value.

If that's the case, there are several tax shelters available. For one, you can refinance. As your house becomes more valuable, you may be able to borrow more against it, especially if your household income has gone up in the interim.

As mentioned, Al and Beth Collins bought a $120,000 house with a $90,000 mortgage. Years later, with the mortgage paid down to $85,000, they decide to refinance. Perhaps interest rates have fallen; perhaps they need to get their hands on a sizable sum.

At that point, the house is appraised at $200,000. Based on the value of the house as well as Al and Beth's income, the bank decides to make a loan of $150,000. Al and Beth can pay off the $85,000 outstanding balance and put the other $65,000 in their pocket. Because that money consists of loan proceeds, it's tax-free.

True, their monthly interest expense will be higher with a $150,000 mortgage, versus their old $85,000 mortgage. However, all the interest will be tax-deductible.

SELL NOW, PAY LATER

Any time you sell a house at a profit, you realize a taxable capital gain. Thanks to another shelter in the tax code, you can defer that tax for many years and, with some planning, you can avoid that tax altogether.

Let's say Al and Beth sell the house they originally bought for $120,000, realizing $200,000 on the sale. That's an $80,000 profit (not bad, considering their down payment was $30,000).

As long as they held the house for more than one year, the profit is treated as a long-term capital gain. As of this writing, the top rate on such gains is 28 percent, lower than the tax rate on income you earn. In the past, capital gains have been treated even more favorably, and that may be the case when you decide to sell your house.

What's more, Al and Beth may not have an $80,000 capital gain. Over the years, they've put a lot of money into their house. Anything that counts as a "capital improvement" adds to their basis.

Translated, a capital improvement is anything that goes beyond regular maintenance to add long-lasting value. Painting your house isn't a capital improvement but enlarging the garage is. So is extensive landscaping work, building a pool, fencing the yard, remodeling the kitchen, converting the basement into a den, and so on.

Capital improvements needn't be major expenses: You can increase the cost basis in your house with smaller expenses such as adding electrical or telephone outlets, blacktopping your driveway, weather-stripping your doors and windows, and adding a layer of insulation to your attic. So keep receipts for all your house-related expenses. Have an envelope marked "improvements" where you keep all your home-related paperwork.

Moreover, you may be able to add some of your furnishings to your cost basis. Suppose you sell your house and the sales contract stipulates that you'll leave behind mirrors, draperies, fireplace accessories, workshop equipment, a lawn mower, and garden equipment. The cost of all these items can be added to your cost basis.

Therefore, when you sell your house, be sure all your "leave-behinds" are included in the contract.

Suppose that Al and Beth have spent $14,250 on such costs while they owned the house and that they have kept the receipts for all this work. Now, their basis in the house—their cost for tax purposes—is $134,250, not $120,000. (This example assumes that the original $120,000 price includes closing costs; if not, those costs also are added to the basis of the house.)

The same reasoning holds true when you sell the house. The "price" may be $200,000 but you may receive only $185,000. That's the net sales price. Moreover, for tax purposes you can deduct any money you spent to help you sell the house (for example, roof repairs) within 90 days of entering into a sales contract. If you spent $1,500, your net sales price falls to $183,500.

Gross sales price	$200,000	
Minus: Fees and commissions	$ 15,000	
Minus: Fix-up costs	$ 1,500	
Net sales price for tax purposes		$183,500
Original purchase price		
(includes closing costs)	$120,000	
Plus: Capital improvements	$ 14,250	
Cost for tax purposes		$134,250
Taxable gain		$ 49,250

As you can see, Al and Beth have a taxable gain of $49,250 on their house, rather than $80,000. Assuming a 28 percent tax rate, they'd owe only $13,790.

PAY LATER RATHER THAN SOONER

Thanks to another risk-free shelter, Al and Beth may not have to pay even that $13,790 in tax. All they have to do is buy another house of greater or equal value than the "adjusted sales price" of the home they sold.

In this example, the adjusted sales price is $183,500, after selling expenses. Therefore, if Al and Beth buy a new home that costs at least $183,500, they'll owe no capital gains tax.

For the purpose of this calculation, the cost of the new house includes all closing costs. For the deferral to kick in, they must purchase the new house within two years of selling the old one. If you're building a new house, you must move in within two years.

Technically, the deferred gain reduces the basis of your new house. For example, Al and Beth spend $230,000 on their new home. The deferred gain is $49,250. Thus, their basis (cost for tax purposes) in the new house is $180,750, not $230,000. That means the deferred tax will be owed when the second home is sold.

What happens if Al and Beth buy a new house for only $150,000? Because that's $33,500 short of the adjusted sales price of the first house, they'll owe tax on a $33,500 gain. The rest of their gain, $15,750, is deferred. The deferral reduces the basis on their new house.

Now, all these numbers may seem confusing, but the basic strategy is simple. If you're a homeowner, keep all records relating to your purchase and subsequent capital improvements. When you sell a house, buy a new one of equal or greater value. No matter how much your homes appreciate, you won't owe any tax.

MORE FEATHERS FOR YOUR EMPTY NEST

You may not keep trading up in the housing market. A common scenario is for a couple to trade down to a smaller house or a rental apartment after the kids leave home and the parents become "empty nesters." Or, the move to a smaller home may take place after retirement. If you can wait until you're age 55 or older, you can use yet another tax shelter.

At age 55 or older, you can exclude up to $125,000 worth of capital gains on a sale of a residence. For example, Al and Beth have traded up from a $120,000 house to a $230,000 house, as explained, deferring the tax but maintaining a cost basis of $180,750. Years later, when they're ready for retirement, they sell their house, receiving an adjusted sales price of $350,000. Thanks to capital improvements, their cost basis has increased to $200,000. After the sale, they move to Florida and buy a condo for $125,000.

Because the cost of their new home ($125,000) is less than the basis they're carrying over ($200,000), they no longer qualify for tax deferral. However, as long as either Al or Beth is at least 55, they can use the age-55 shelter.

Without this shelter, they'd owe:

Adjusted sales price	$350,000
Minus: cost basis	$200,000
Taxable capital gain	$150,000

If you assume a 28 percent tax on the gain, they'd owe $42,000. However, the age-55 shelter allows them to exclude $125,000 worth of gain. Now, their taxable gain is only $25,000 and they'd owe only $7,000 in tax. This shelter saves Al and Beth $35,000.

Look at it in another light. Starting as young marrieds, they buy a $120,000 house with a $30,000 down payment. Over the next 40 years or so, they trade up and enjoy a valuation increase to a $350,000 house. After they cash out, they owe only $7,000 in tax and they still own a $125,000 condo.

Of course, there are strings attached to the age-55 exclusion. It applies only to the sale of a home that you've used as a principal residence at least three of the last five years. (Similarly, the deferral of taxable gain, described earlier, applies only to a principal residence.) Plus, it's a once-in-a-lifetime tax break. If you've used it once, you can't use it again.

This can be a trap in case of remarriage. Suppose Al dies after he and Beth have used this shelter, and Beth marries Charles, a widower. Charles lives in a house he's owned for years, which he now wants to sell. Because he's now married to Beth, and Beth already has used the age-55 shelter, Charles can't use it.

Unromantic though it may sound, Charles is better off selling his house first, marrying Beth second.

VANISHING ACT

Therefore, the over-55 tax break can shelter up to $125,000 worth of capital gains from housing appreciation. If your total appreciation, as you trade up through the housing market, is $125,000 or less, you're completely sheltered. If your appreciation is greater, you can shelter part or most of your gains.

But there's another way to shelter housing gains, no matter how great the appreciation. This shelter is as basic as they come: hang onto your house until you die.

Suppose, for example, that Al and Beth retain ownership of their house through their retirement. Maybe they buy a small apartment in Florida, where they spend their winters. At Al's death, he leaves his share of the primary residence to Beth. In turn, Beth moves to Florida full time and rents out the house that had been their primary residence.

Eventually, Beth dies. All her assets, including the one-time primary residence, pass to her children, Ed and Fran.

Here's where the tax break comes in. Under current tax law, assets that change hands at death get a step-up in basis. The new basis is the asset's value at the time of death, or six months afterwards.

The house in question, for example, had a cost basis of $200,000. Assume that they owned the house jointly. Therefore, at Al's death, Al and Beth both have a cost basis of $100,000.

At Al's death, the property automatically passes to Beth, as his co-owner. Beth, as the executor of Al's estate, has to have the house valued. She hires an appraiser who puts the current value at

$300,000. Therefore, Al's half of the house, which passes to Beth, has a stepped-up basis of $150,000.

Thus, here is Beth's position:

Cost basis	$200,000	
Beth's half		$100,000
Value at time of Al's death	$300,000	
Stepped-up basis of his half		$150,000
Beth's new basis, as sole owner		$250,000

Suppose she now sells her house for $300,000. She'll have a taxable gain of $50,000. If she's over 55 and chooses to use the age-55 tax break, the $125,000 exclusion will shelter all the gain, wiping out all taxes on the past appreciation.

Suppose, however, that Beth chooses not to sell. She might live in the house until she dies or she might move to a smaller place while renting it out. At the time of her death, the house goes to her children.

Acting as co-executors, they get a new appraisal, which values the house at $400,000. That value becomes the new basis for the house they now own. If they sell the house next week or next month or next year, for $400,000, they'll owe no tax. All of Al and Beth's housing appreciation, deferred over the years, is never taxed.

If Ed and Fran sell their parents' house for $415,000, they'll have a $15,000 taxable gain. If they sell the house for $395,000, they'll actually have a $5,000 loss, which they can deduct, despite all the past appreciation. (It's possible that an estate tax obligation will be triggered when Beth dies, leaving a $400,000 house and, presumably, other assets. See Chapter 22 for details on estate tax shelters.)

ON THE HOUSE

That's how to use your house or a series of houses as a tax shelter: Buy well so that your residence appreciates. You can take loans against your home equity, receiving the proceeds, tax-free. As long as your mortgages, second mortgages, and your home equity loans are secured by your home, the interest is tax-deductible (subject to the limits mentioned previously).

If you sell your house, the gain can be deferred, as long as you keep trading up. When you reach age 55, you can cash out and shelter up to $125,000 worth of appreciation. Or, you can stay on the housing ladder until your death, completely avoiding taxes on the built-up appreciation.

It's possible that the tax law will change, requiring some tax on this built-up appreciation. However, since a disastrous attempt in the 1970s, Congress hasn't shown much interest in this area. Moreover, any attempt to tax capital gains at death may well exclude principal residences or have a specified exemption (for example, $125,000 worth of gains might be untaxed).

If the law changes, you may be able to plan around it. For now, trading up in the housing market will shelter you from Washington's as well as from nature's storms.

SUMMING UP

- When you sell your home at a profit, you'll have a taxable gain.
- That gain can be reduced if you keep track of all your home improvements and add them to your cost basis.
- The tax on your gain can be deferred if you purchase a new home of greater or equal value within two years.
- You can trade up through the housing market, continuing to defer tax on the built-up gains.
- After you reach age 55, you can exclude up to $125,000 worth of capital gains related to your principal residence.
- Under current law, if you die with built-up gains, those gains will be effectively wiped out. Your heirs can sell the house and owe no tax.
- As long as you're on the housing ladder, you may be able to tap your unrealized equity through tax-free loans.

15 Minding Your Own Business
The Tax Advantages of Working for Yourself

You shouldn't start a business to save taxes. You want to make money, of course. Beyond that, you want to control your own fate and not depend on someone else for raises or promotions. When you start your own business, even a sideline business, you're the boss.

Nevertheless, the tax benefits help. When you're truly pursuing a profit, many of the things you do become deductible expenses. Restaurant meals become business meals, ballpark excursions become business entertaining, your personal computer becomes a business machine. As long as you keep good records, you may be entitled to substantial deductions, which will reduce or eliminate the tax you owe on your business income.

FIRM FOUNDATION

The first decision you need to make when you become a business owner is the structure you'll use. In essence, you can do business as a sole proprietor, a partnership, or a corporation.

The simplest structure is a sole proprietorship. Laurie Bryan, for example, decides to go into the hair ornament business. She buys materials, assembles them in her home, and sells them to stores. All she needs to do is keep track of her business income and her business-related expenses. When she files her tax return, she fills out a Schedule C, for self-employment income.

Then Laurie meets Herb Cooper, who has an idea for a line of hats. Laurie and Herb think their product lines will fit together well, so they form a partnership, Bry-Coop Associates. They sign a partnership agreement, stating that income and expenses will be split 50–50.

Now, Bry-Coop fills out a partnership tax return. The partnership, though, owes no income tax. Instead, partnership profits are divided between the partners, according to the partnership agreement. If Bry-Coop shows a net profit of $20,000 for 1994, Laurie and Herb each report $10,000 worth of income on their individual tax returns.

INC SPOTS

As their business grows, Laurie and Herb rent office space and hire employees. Now, they have some new concerns. What if an employee or a visiting salesperson trips and suffers a serious injury? A suit might be brought against the Bry-Coop partnership. If so, and there's a damages award, Bry-Coop will be liable. Both Laurie and Herb, as partners, are fully liable for the partnership's debts.

Therefore, they incorporate Bry-Coop, Inc. Today, there are few tax advantages to incorporation. Laurie and Herb, if they decide to incorporate, will do so primarily for the limited liability that corporate shareholders enjoy. A suit against Bry-Coop, Inc. may not threaten their personal assets. As partners, everything they own might be lost because of partnership debt or liability.

Now, Laurie and Herb each own 50 percent of the corporate stock. The corporation pays each of them a salary for the work they perform; any other employees also receive a salary. As employees, Laurie and Herb report their salaries as compensation when they file income tax, just as all employees do.

But for Laurie and Herb, things don't end there. Bry-Coop, Inc. must file a corporate income tax return. What's more, any profits are subject to corporate income tax: federal tax, probably state tax, and perhaps local income tax, too.

WHEN ZERO IS A PLUS

One way to avoid or minimize this corporate income tax is to "zero it out." Say Bry-Coop earns $100,000 in 1994. If Bry-Coop pays $50,000 apiece to Laurie and Herb, as salaries, Bry-Coop will wind up with no net income and owe no corporate tax while Laurie and Herb will each report $50,000 in compensation.

Unfortunately, life isn't that easy. At the beginning of the year, Laurie and Herb won't know exactly how much money Bry-Coop will earn, so they can't set their salaries precisely. Also, they may not want to strip Bry-Coop of all its operating capital.

Therefore, they can use a salary-plus-bonus arrangement. They can set their annual salaries at, say, $40,000 a year. At the end of the year, when it seems as though Bry-Coop will wind up with an additional $20,000, they can declare a $10,000 bonus for each co-owner. Again, Bry-Coop will be zeroed out and owe no corporate income tax.

As you might expect, the IRS does not like this little game. On audit, the IRS may say that the $10,000 bonuses weren't really bonuses paid as compensation to employees. Instead, they really were corporate profits distributed to the co-owners. Under this theory, the $10,000 bonuses are considered dividends, a tax disaster.

Why are dividends so deadly? Because the corporation can't deduct them. Here, Bry-Coop would have to pay corporate income tax on its $20,000 profit, then Laurie and Herb each have to recognize $10,000 in taxable income. In essence, dividends are taxed twice.

There's a better way to zero out your corporate tax obligation: You can establish a corporate-sponsored retirement plan, such as those described in Chapters 1 to 3. Contributions are fully deductible, as long as they conform to limits set out in the tax code. Those deductions can reduce or eliminate the company's taxable income, yet the employees (including owner-employees) are not immediately taxed on contributions made on their behalf.

"S" AS IN SMART

Another way to get around the corporate income tax is to elect "S corporation" status. With an S corporation, taxation is similar to that of a partnership. Any profits are passed through, to be divided by the shareholders according to their stake in the company. The corporate income tax doesn't apply.

To qualify as an S corporation, certain criteria must be met. You can't have two classes of stock; for example, you can't have more than 35 shareholders, you can't have foreign shareholders, and only certain trusts can qualify as shareholders. Most very small businesses, though, can meet these qualifications, so making an S corporation election usually makes sense.

If you want to sell your S corporation in the future, have that stock redeemed by the corporation, or receive liquidating proceeds from the corporation, the money received will be taxed only once, avoiding the corporate income tax. Long term, that can be a huge advantage.

Once you have an S corporation, there's a certain amount of planning you can do. Laurie, who owns 50 percent of Bry-Coop, might give away 20 percent of the shares to her children. Then, that portion of the corporate profits will be passed through to them, in their low tax brackets. Also, Laurie has managed to get those shares out of her taxable estate, which may be a sizable tax advantage in the future (see Chapter 22).

Remember, even though an S corporation is taxed like a partnership, it's still a corporation. Thus, shareholders' personal assets are protected from claims against the business.

That doesn't mean that all small businesses should be S corporations. S corporations can't get a full deduction for medical costs, while a regular C corporation permits you to pay your health expenses with pre-tax dollars. It's true that you are liable for corporate income tax with a C corporation, but that corporation won't have any income to tax if you can legitimately pay out most or all of your profits in salary. So check with your CPA on the advantages of C versus S corporations.

LOSS LEADERS

Not all start-up businesses make money right away. Some hugely successful enterprises such as *Sports Illustrated* magazine suffered through years of losses before turning profitable.

If your fledgling business runs up losses, you naturally will want to deduct all your business-related expenses. The IRS may not permit loss deductions, however, especially if the activity is something that seems like fun. For an activity classed as a "hobby," deductions can't exceed your income from the activity, and they might not be deductible at all.

Take the case of a writer who claimed to be researching a book about the perfect steak. His "research" took him all over the world, to some of the world's finest restaurants. Along the way, he was taking $25,000 worth of business expense deductions each year. The IRS, though, had a beef with him: This very creative writer was hit with a bill for back taxes, interest, and penalties.

Not all taxpayer attempts to write off pleasurable pursuits are doomed to failure. David K., for example, a musical and theatrical promoter, supported his wife Cheryl's efforts to break into show business, financing a rock band with four professional musicians and Cheryl singing lead. These efforts led to a lot of expense but little income. After several years, the IRS disallowed the deductions.

However, David and Cheryl fought the case in Tax Court, where they won. The Court found that David, and especially Cheryl, had spent considerable time on this project. An option for a recording contract had been obtained; when that option lapsed, the band had disbanded. Thus, the Court felt that Cheryl had sincerely tried to launch her singing career.

Similarly, the IRS challenged the deductions of Stella W., a would-be artist who never showed a profit in 10 years. The Tax Court sided with Stella, finding that she had been a full-time artist who had exhibited her work and won several fellowships.

In essence, that's what the Court looks for: a reasonable indication that you might make a profit at some point. The more business-like you are, with separate books and records, and the greater your level of skill, the better your chance of convincing the IRS that you are in a bona fide business.

According to the tax code, if you show a profit in two out of every five consecutive years, you're presumed to be in business. (For horse-related activities, it's two out of every seven years.) So don't be greedy and claim losses every year if you engage in an activity that might be considered a hobby. Every second or third year, report enough income and cut your reported expenses to show a taxable profit.

What's the difference? Business losses are fully deductible, generally on Schedule C (Schedule F for farming). Hobby expenses are deductible only to the extent of your income from that activity, which you also must report. Plus, those hobby expenses likely will have to be reported as miscellaneous deductions on Schedule A, where you itemize deductions. Those expenses are deductible only to the extent they exceed 2 percent of adjusted gross income, so some or all of them might not be deductible.

CASH COWS BEAT HOBBY HORSES

Many hobby-versus-business cases are "gentleman farmer" situations. A Hollywood director grows grapes on his estate in the Napa Valley in California; a Manhattan executive raises horses at his country retreat in Dutchess County. Naturally, the IRS tends to doubt whether these are bona fide businesses.

If you have the means, there's an audit-proof way to beat the taxman: pay cash. Buy your real estate and your equipment. Don't borrow or pay rent.

What does this accomplish? You sharply reduce your operating costs by eliminating debt service or lease payments. With expenses down, you can show a profit even if you sell only a few cases of wine or a few foals each year. You likely will pay a few hundred dollars a year in tax, but the net effect is that you can shelter most of your income with expenses that otherwise would be nondeductible. And, if you show an occasional loss, it likely will be deductible, after several years of reported profits.

If you need cash down the road, you can borrow against your property, tax-free. When it's time to sell, any profit will be a tax-advantaged capital gain.

DECLARING YOUR INDEPENDENCE

Another tax question facing the self-employed is whether you're an independent contractor or an employee in the eyes of the IRS. If you're a salesperson, for example, and you do most of your work for one company, your status may be unclear.

The IRS prefers to call workers employees. Then the employer is responsible for withholding income and payroll taxes. The IRS gets its money up front. Workers generally prefer to be independent contractors (that is, self-employed) because more can be written off for retirement savings and job-related expenses.

Taxpayers have beaten the IRS on this issue. Exotic dancers in Dallas worked at one establishment so the IRS contended they were employees. However, as it turned out, the dancers paid the bar $20 to $40 a night for the right to work there. (They made their money in tips, presumably enough to justify the initial business expense.) So a court held that they were independent contractors.

If you're in some other line of work, how can you prove your independence? Have several customers or clients or sources of income. Send in invoices for each piece of work you do.

Most of all, the contractor-versus-employee question turns on the matter of control. If you can come and go, work at your own speed, use your own methods, and work without supervision, you're more likely to be considered an independent contractor.

SUMMING UP

- Many business owners incorporate to limit their liability.
- Corporations, though, are subject to the corporate income tax.
- For small companies, an S corporation election provides limited liability as well as no exposure to the corporate income tax.

- To avoid having your business classed as a hobby (which limits tax deductions), you need to show a legitimate attempt to earn a profit.
- If there's a doubt about whether you're an employee or an independent contractor, evidence that you're in control of your work schedule can help you establish your independence, which offers more tax deductions.

16 Home Sweet Home Office

How to Deduct Your Household Expenses

Early in 1993, *The New York Times* reported on George B., owner of an import business based in Red Bank, N.J. George runs the business from the sun porch of his house, which occupies 10 percent of the house. Therefore, George takes a deduction for 10 percent of his household expenses.

For example, the annual cost of maintenance and repairs, such as fixing the electrical system or unclogging heating ducts, might be $1,500. If so, George takes a $150 deduction. If he pays $2,500 a year for utilities, he gets to deduct $250. On a $600 homeowner's insurance policy, the deduction would be $60. And so on. Altogether, George gets to cut his taxes by hundreds of dollars a year by maintaining a home office. If you qualify for a home office deduction, you can enjoy similar tax savings.

A ROOM OF ONE'S OWN

There are two main criteria to meet if you want to qualify for this deduction. First, you need to have a portion of your home that you use "exclusively" for business. Typically, that will be a separate room but a section of a room may be appropriate in some cases. Don't use that space for anything else—it shouldn't double as a guest bedroom or as a TV room for your kids.

The second requirement is that you use your home office "regularly" for business. There are no hard-and-fast rules for this, but you're asking for trouble if you claim a room that you use once a month for business is a home office. The more you use your home office, the better.

Meeting the regular-and-exclusive test is necessary for a home office deduction, but it's not enough. If you're employed at your company's headquarters, for example, and keep a room in your home to work nights and weekends, you probably won't be eligible for the write-off. To qualify for this tax shelter, you need to use your space either (1) as your principal place of business or (2) as a place to meet with clients in the normal course of business.

NOT WHAT THE DOCTOR ORDERED

The IRS does not like the idea of taxpayers claiming a home office and deducting normal living expenses. For years, it hounded Dr. Nader Soliman, a Virginia anaesthesiologist, suffering two court setbacks before triumphing in the Supreme Court in 1993. As a result, it is much tougher to sustain a home office deduction.

Dr. Soliman worked at three local hospitals but did not have an office in any of them. Thus, he used the spare bedroom of his home as an office, keeping records and making phone calls. He claimed deductions for a home office, claims the Tax Court, and the Appellate Court upheld.

The Supreme Court disagreed. According to its opinion, because Dr. Soliman took care of his patients at the hospitals, the hospitals were his primary work places, not the home office. Besides, he spent only 10 to 15 hours a week in his office, much less than the 30 to 35 hours spent in hospitals.

So there's a new test for home office deductions. You can claim an office as your primary place of business if you do most of your work there. If your "most important function" is performed somewhere else, you'll have a hard time making a deduction stand up. That might affect contractors, repairmen, house painters, and others.

In case your situation isn't clear-cut, keep a record of the time spent inside your home office and outside, to back up your claims. Try to build an argument that the work done at home (for example, research) is the most important function of your business.

If you don't meet the "primary place of business" criteria, the only way you can get a home office deduction is to regularly see clients, patients, or customers there in the course of business. If you can meet with people in your home office, do so. A doctor who regularly treats patients in a home office would qualify, even if another office is used more frequently.

SQUARE DEALS

If you meet the standards for deducting a home office, you have to do some math. Figure out the size of your home and the size of your home office. If your home has 1,500 square feet, for example, and you use a room with 180 square feet as a home office, you're entitled to a 12 percent deduction—you can deduct 12 percent of all your household expenses. You also can depreciate 12 percent of your house. That is, if your house (not the land) is worth $100,000, you get a $12,000 deduction, spread over the 27.5-year period specified by the tax code.

On some expenses, though, you're probably better off not taking the 12 percent deduction. For example, if you work extensively at home, your business-phone expenses probably are more than 12 percent of the total. So install a separate line for a full write-off.

Good records, naturally, are a key to sustaining a home office deduction. But how can you avoid an audit altogether if you take this deduction? Some experts say it helps to take a photo of your home office and attach it to your tax return, along with an explanation of how the office is used.

The IRS is so determined to stamp out abuses in this area that it has introduced a separate Form 8829 that must be attached to your tax return if you claim a home office deduction. Naturally, filing this form makes your return more visible, but you're not automatically audit bait. Don't be intimidated. If you're entitled to home office deductions, take them.

DEDUCT, DON'T DEPRECIATE

When you have your own business, you can deduct expenses beyond a home office. For example, you're allowed to deduct office equipment, as long as business use is over 50 percent. (If you use a home computer 75 percent of the time it's in use for your business, you get a 75 percent deduction.) So keep a log of how often your equipment is used for business versus personal pursuits.

Technically, you're supposed to write off such expenses over a period of years, depending on the type of equipment. However, you can take immediate first-year writeoffs on $10,000 worth of business equipment a year. (As of this writing, an increase to $25,000 had been proposed.)You can take this deduction whether or not you qualify for a home office deduction.

RECREATION ROOM

If there's any area the IRS looks at as intensively as home office deductions, it's travel and entertainment (T&E) expenses. The more T&E deductions you claim, the more audit-prone you are. So it pays to know the ground rules before you take deductions.

To be deductible, T&E must be directly related to, or at least associated with, the active conduct of your business. Auto Zapper & Towing, Inc., for example, a California company that repossesses cars and boats, relies on banks and other lenders for its business. In 1988, the company hired three buses to take Auto Zapper employees and lenders' employees for a weekend in Las Vegas. The company deducted the cost, over $9,000, as T&E.

Even though the weekend went well and Auto Zapper reaped more repos, the Tax Court foreclosed the deductions. There were no scheduled business meetings, nothing directly related to Auto Zapper's business. Goodwill alone isn't enough. For T&E to be deductible, there has to be an active effort to promote business. And you need to keep a log that shows your T&E effort.

If you take someone out to dinner or to a ballgame, be sure to talk business before, during, or after the meal or game. Write down the details. You'll likely be entitled to a deduction.

The rules on deducting business travel costs and expenses incurred while away from home are complex, especially if you mix in some nonbusiness activities. Your best bet is to keep a detailed log, showing as much business activity as you can, and ask your tax preparer what you can legitimately deduct.

If you're traveling out of the United States on business-and-pleasure, try to keep your trips to less than a week, because the deductibility rules are more generous for short trips.

SPOUSE CALLS

For T&E that involves your spouse, you'll naturally prefer to write off the total cost, but spousal deductions are tough to sustain. You need to show that your spouse performed substantial business services in order to deduct the expense. For example, deductions have been allowed for a spouse who took care of her diabetic husband, who was traveling on business. Also, a spouse who was a professional secretary and who performed secretarial services on a trip was deemed "essential."

Or, suppose you invite two customers (not social acquaintances) to your country club. Although you spend some time swimming and dining, most of the day is spent talking business. Your spouse entertains the other spouses. Your activities are directly related to your business while your spouse's are associated with your business, so all the costs are deductible. (It will strengthen your case if you actually negotiate some business that day and have records to prove it.)

Similarly, home entertainment may be deductible, including gatherings the uninitiated may call parties. The key is to make a bona fide attempt to conduct business at these occasions. If you're a professional photographer, say, ask your guests if they have a wedding coming up, or if they need head-and-shoulders shots for company publicity. Ask if they know anyone who might be in the market for a photographer. Write down what was discussed and be sure to follow up afterwards. Again, your position will be much stronger if you actually get some substantial business from these occasions.

SPLIT ENDS

As your business grows and begins to earn substantial amounts of money, more tax shelters become available. For example, take the low-income housing tax credit, described in Chapter 11. C corporations may be able to use much greater amounts of these credits than individual taxpayers can, in addition to using the passive losses to offset business income.

Another opportunity lies in the area of "split-dollar" life insurance arrangements, in which a C corporation pays part or all of the premiums. In the most common situation, the company pays the entire premium. The employee (or you, the owner-employee) receives a taxable benefit, which is taxed according to the insurer's term life insurance rates. A 50-year-old male, for example, might have imputed income of $1.45 per $1,000 of insurance. Thus, your company could buy a $300,000 insurance policy on your life and you'd have $435 in imputed income, so you'd owe around $170 in extra tax. You get a substantial insurance benefit for a few tax dollars.

In this type of split-dollar arrangement, the company would pay the premiums but would carry the cumulative premiums paid as a balance sheet asset. In case of your death, your company would be reimbursed for the premiums it paid, while the balance goes to your beneficiaries. In addition, the company would have access to the cash value, up to the amount of premiums paid.

A variation, "reverse split-dollar," calls for the owner-employee to own the cash value while the company gets the death benefit. Suppose Russell Morgan, 45 years old, wants to retire in 20 years. In the meantime, he wants his company to have $1 million worth of life insurance protection in case of his untimely death.

Over the next 20 years, Russell's company, Morgan Metals, pays annual $15,000 insurance premiums to keep that $1 million policy in force. Russell pays $3,000 per year. After 20 years, and a total of

$360,000 in premium payments ($18,000 times 20), the policy's cash value likely will be over $500,000, thanks to tax-free compounding.

Now, Russell can retire and borrow, say, $40,000 or $50,000 per year, tax-free, as retirement income. Thus, Russell protects his company (that is, protects his family's greatest asset) and provides for his own retirement without having to provide similar benefits for all of Morgan Metals' employees.

Split-dollar and reverse split-dollar strategies are complex, with the latter especially prone to IRS scrutiny. You'll need to work with a tax pro on these and other corporate tax shelters.

SUMMING UP

- To get home office deductions, you need to have a separate place in your home that's used regularly and exclusively for business.

- Furthermore, your home office must be your principal place of business or must be used regularly for meetings with customers.

- Travel and entertainment expenses must be related to your business and must be fully documented if they're to be deductible.

- Successful corporations can use tax shelters such as split-dollar life insurance, which provides low-cost insurance to owner-employees, and reverse split-dollar, which can serve as a supplementary retirement plan.

17 Itemize Without Pulling the Audit Trigger

Maximize Your Itemized Deductions

One basic decision facing all taxpayers is whether or not to "itemize" deductions on Schedule A of Form 1040. If you decide not to itemize, you'll get a standard deduction, available to all taxpayers. Only if you decide that your itemized deductions substantially exceed the standard deduction should you take the trouble—and the increased audit risk—of itemizing.

In 1993, the standard deduction was $3,700 for a single taxpayer, $6,200 for joint returns. That deduction goes up each year, to keep pace with inflation. With inflation currently running around 3 percent per year, the standard deduction for a joint return will be about $6,400 in 1994, $6,600 in 1995, and so on.

Therefore, your itemized deductions should be clearly above the standard to make itemizing worthwhile. If you estimate your itemized deductions at $6,500 in 1994, for example, your extra $100 in deductions will save you about $30 in taxes. That's hardly worth the time, effort, and exposure of itemizing.

How can you tell if it's worth taking the time and effort of itemizing until you've already taken that time and effort, to come up with a number for your itemized deductions? There's a shortcut you can use to quickly gauge whether or not you're over the limit.

For most people in most years, three categories of itemized deductions make up the lion's share: mortgage interest, state and local taxes, and charitable contributions. When you're preparing your tax return, you generally can estimate those in a few minutes from bank records, estimated tax payments, W-2 statements, local tax statements, and so on. If those items alone add up to $7,000 or more, you should itemize. (The threshold is around $4,000 for single filers.) If not, save yourself some headaches and take the standard deduction.

Once you've decided to itemize, there are some strategies you can use to increase your tax shelter.

BUNCH YOUR MEDICAL DEDUCTIONS

Medical costs are deductible only if they're over 7.5 percent of your adjusted gross income (AGI), so your first step is to estimate your AGI for the current year. Start with last year's tax return—your AGI is the last number on the bottom of the first side of Form 1040. Then make the appropriate adjustment, based on whether you think this year's AGI will be greater or lower.

For example, Joe and Jean Lewis had a $75,000 AGI in 1993. They estimate 1994 AGI a bit higher, around $80,000. They can deduct medical costs that exceed 7.5 percent of their AGI, or $6,000. That is, if their total medical costs are $8,000, they can deduct $2,000. Some tax planning for medical expenses should take place at year-end (see Chapter 20), but there are also things they can do throughout the year.

For example, if Jean suffers from an allergy or a respiratory condition, her physician may recommend that she add central air-conditioning to her house, along with a dehumidifier. Jean should get a note from her doctor as well as before-and-after appraisals of her house. If the expense of the installation costs exceeds the increase in value, the difference is considered a medical expense.

Joe and Jean install a central air-conditioning and dehumidifier system in their house, spending $15,000. Their house is appraised at

$140,000 before and $150,000 after. Thus, of the $15,000 they spent, $10,000 is considered a capital cost, adding to their basis in the house, while the other $5,000 is a current medical expense.

Remember, though, that the expense is not deductible—it's "wasted"—if total medical expenses don't top the 7.5 percent threshold. So channel your elective expenses into every other year, or every third year, or into a year when you have unavoidable major medical costs, to make the most of this deduction.

Suppose Joe and Jean, with an estimated $80,000 AGI, have a medical emergency early in 1994. They're insured, but they wind up $5,000 out-of-pocket because of their deductible, co-insurance payments, and nondeductible items. Because it seems almost certain they'll be over the 7.5 percent ($6,000) threshold, they should install the air-conditioner and dehumidifier system in that year.

As long as they can afford it, they should schedule elective medical expenses throughout 1994 and incur other medically necessary expenses. If necessary, they can charge expenses on credit cards in 1994, for an immediate deduction, while the bills can be paid off over a long time period.

TAXING MATTERS

The next item on Schedule A is "Taxes you paid." In essence, you can deduct state and local income taxes, as well as real estate property taxes, paid during the calendar year. That includes any back taxes you paid for prior years, because of tax audits.

There really isn't much you can do in this area, except make sure your outstanding taxes are paid up by year-end. If you buy or sell your house, make sure your closing statement includes a breakdown of which party is paying how much of the property tax, so you can take the appropriate deductions.

EARN 19 PERCENT AFTER-TAX, RISK-FREE

Interest deductions, which appear next on Schedule A, are easy to keep straight. Interest on loans secured by your personal residence and a second home is deductible, as described in Chapter 13. Consumer interest is not deductible. Therefore, if you have home equity, you're better off with a home equity loan than with other types of credit lines. Just be sure you don't borrow more than you can afford, and thus put your house in jeopardy.

If you have outstanding credit-card debt, or other types of personal loans, you're getting no tax shelter at all because the interest is not deductible. Therefore, your investment strategy should be focused in one direction: repay those loans.

Don't buy CDs, don't put cash into money market funds; don't invest in stocks. Put every extra penny you have for savings and investment into repayment of that consumer debt.

Why? Because repaying a debt is the same as earning the interest rate on that debt. Some credit cards charge as much as 19 percent per year. When you pay down your outstanding balance, and avoid paying 19 percent interest, you're effectively earning 19 percent.

What's more, because the interest is not sheltered, avoiding the interest payment is the same as earning 19 percent (or 12 percent or 15 percent or whatever) after-tax. Without any risk. There's no other investment that can provide that kind of return, risk-free. So pay off your outstanding credit lines before you do anything else. (As mentioned, you may want to leave tax-deductible home equity lines outstanding, if your tax bracket is high and the interest rate is low.)

CLEAN HOUSE, CLEAN UP

The rules on charitable contributions are similarly straightforward. You get to deduct what you give to qualified organizations, which includes most schools, hospitals, public charities, and so forth. If you do some type of volunteer work, keep records of your out-of-pocket expenses (for example, auto expenses, phone calls, stationery, postage), which are deductible.

Once a year, go through your house and give away stuff you no longer need, such as books and clothing. Get a receipt that indicates what you gave and the items' condition. This is a fairly painless way of getting a deduction worth hundreds of dollars each year, while you clean house at the same time. As long as you keep the value of this deduction below $500 per year, you won't have to fill out Form 8283, explaining what you donated.

DONATE APPRECIATED SECURITIES INSTEAD OF CASH

For best results when you're making charitable contributions, donate appreciated securities. This will enable you to avoid tax on the capital gains.

Say you have mutual funds you bought for $200 and now are worth $1,000. A sale would trigger an $800 capital gain. You'd probably owe around $225 in taxes, leaving you with only $775 to give to your favorite charity, your alma mater. That leaves your alma mater with only $775 and gives you a $775 tax deduction.

Instead, you can just give the $1,000 worth of mutual funds to the school. You'd get a full $1,000 tax deduction and your $800 taxable capital gain would disappear.

As for your alma mater, it can sell the donated mutual fund shares and collect the full $1,000. Because of its tax-exempt, nonprofit status, the school won't owe any tax on the sale. In essence, this strategy gives both you and the school a $1,000 benefit on an asset with a net value of $775.

	Sell, Then Donate	Donate the Shares
You bought mutual funds for	$ 200	$ 200
Shares are now worth	$1,000	$1,000
A sale triggers a capital gain of	$ 800	no sale
@28%, you owe tax of	$ 224	0
After-tax proceeds	$ 776	
Charitable recipient receives	$ 776	$1,000
You get a tax deduction of	$ 776	$1,000

If you need help with the mechanics of donating appreciated securities, ask your broker to handle it. Or contact the charity: The people there will know how to deal with the transaction.

There are a few caveats to consider before giving appreciated property. First, you won't get the full deduction unless you've held the asset for at least one year. Say you bought stock at $600 in April and gave it to the March of Dimes the next December, when its market price was $1,000. You'd get a $600 deduction, not a $1,000 deduction.

Also, you can deduct long-term capital gain property worth only up to 30 percent of your adjusted gross income (AGI). Say your AGI in 1994 is $50,000. You're limited to $15,000 worth of tax deductions for long-term capital gain property on your 1994 tax return.

What if you miscalculate and donate $25,000 worth of such property? You can deduct $15,000 for 1994 and carry the excess $10,000 forward, to deduct within the next five years.

Another problem concerns the alternative minimum tax (AMT). The untaxed appreciation is a preference item for purposes of the AMT. If you have enough tax preference items, including state and local income tax deductions as well as accelerated depreciation, you'll run into the AMT and your tax planning may be wasted. So ask your tax preparer about your AMT situation before giving away significant amounts of appreciated property.

Giving away appreciated assets to charity can make sense but giving away depreciated assets does not. Suppose you have a stock you bought for $1,000 that's now worth $600. If you sell the stock, you'll get a $400 capital loss; then you can donate the $600 sale proceeds in cash. That's better than giving away the $600 stock and winding up with no capital loss to deduct.

LEASE IT OR LOSE IT

Other itemized deductions don't provide much in the way of tax-planning opportunities until you get to the final section, Employee Business Expenses and Other Expenses. You can deduct these expenses over 2 percent of your AGI.

The employee business expense deduction may be substantial, especially for auto and travel expenses, as long as you keep track of your job-related travel. Here's a strategy you might pursue if (1) you drive a personal car extensively on business, unreimbursed by your employer; and (2) you're thinking about taking out a large auto loan to buy a new car.

The interest on such a loan won't be deductible no matter how much you drive a car on business. You can convert nondeductible interest to deductible interest by using a home equity loan instead of an auto loan. Then, the interest will be deductible, provided you're under the $100,000 limit.

But you may not want to use a home equity loan to buy a car. Or, you may not have home equity against which you can borrow. In those cases, look into leasing rather than buying. For example, if you pay $300 a month to lease a car and one third of your driving is for business, you can deduct $100 worth of lease payments per month, in addition to one third of normal operating and maintenance costs. In effect, leasing allows you to get a partial deduction of your financing and depreciation costs.

In addition to auto expense, you can deduct the cost of a home computer, if you can demonstrate it's used to meet your job responsibilities and education expenses necessary to maintain your professional skills. If you're looking for a new job, some of those expenses may be deductible as well.

Another category of expense under this heading relates to investments and money management. Tax preparation falls in this area, along with safe deposit rental (if it holds investment-related documents) and investment advisory fees.

These expenses are lumped together and deducted to the extent they exceed 2 percent of AGI. Thus, the best strategy is to try to cluster expenses to top the 2 percent threshold. You might want to play a defer-and-accelerate game, bunching these deductions every other year to increase the deductible amounts.

SUMMING UP

- Before you take the time and trouble to itemize deductions, get a rough idea of the total you'll wind up with. Unless you'll be substantially over the standard deduction amount, itemizing isn't worth the added effort and audit risk.

- Most itemized deductions are in the charitable, mortgage interest, and local tax categories, so look there first for an estimate.
- Bunch medical expenses to exceed the threshold, which is 7.5 percent of AGI. If you incur heavy expenses early in a year, purchase elective medical procedures and equipment that year.
- If you have outstanding credit card debt, pay it off before making any other investments. Such prepayments generate double-digit returns, after-tax, risk-free.
- Donate unwanted property each year—you can claim a deduction of up to $500 without filing Form 8283.
- Donate appreciated securities instead of cash to avoid the tax on capital gains.
- If you use a car on business, unreimbursed by your employer, you can increase your deduction by leasing instead of buying with an auto loan.

18 Sweet Charity

Why Charitable Remainder Trusts Are Super Shelters

Giving appreciated assets rather than cash to charity is a savvy tax move, as explained in the last section. Moreover, if your appreciated assets are larger in scale, and you have charitable intentions to match, you can use one of the most powerful shelters in the tax code. If your untaxed appreciation runs into five figures, certainly into six figures, you can create a charitable remainder trust (CRT).

Here's the basic outline. You set up a trust and donate your appreciated assets to the trust. For your donation, you get a charitable contribution. The trust, in turn, pays income to designated beneficiaries, for a period of time. After that time period, whatever is left in the trust (the remainder) goes to a charity or charities of your choice.

Why is this such a powerful tax shelter? An example can illustrate its advantages.

Henry Davis started investing in mutual funds 30 years ago. He chose funds that bought small-company growth stocks. Over the years, he has built up $100,000 worth of shares in such funds.

Now Henry is ready to retire. He's looking for income to supplement his company pension and social security. His mutual funds, however, pay virtually no dividends because the companies in which they invest tend to use profits to build their business rather than pay dividends.

Henry could sell his stock funds and reinvest in bond funds, increasing his income. However, a check of his records shows that his basis in these funds—the money he has actually invested—is only $10,000. If he sells his stock funds, he'll have a $90,000 capital gain. Assuming a 35 percent tax rate (federal and state), he'll wind up owing $31,500 in taxes, leaving him only $68,500 to invest in bonds.

Instead, Henry sets up a CRT. He and his wife Ilene are devoted churchgoers who generally make substantial contributions. So the church is named the charitable beneficiary of the CRT.

After the CRT is established, Henry transfers his stock funds to it. Because it's a charitable trust, there are no gift tax consequences.

The CRT then sells the stock fund shares and collects $100,000. No capital gains tax is due. Just as in the case of a contribution of appreciated securities, the capital gains tax obligation disappears when you donate assets to a charity. Therefore, the CRT can invest the full $100,000 in bond funds. That's 45 percent more than the $68,500 Henry would have had if he had sold the shares, paid the tax, and reinvested the balance.

Henry sells shares for		$100,000
Taxable gain is	$90,000	
Total of taxes due @35%		$ 31,500
Amount left for Henry to reinvest		$ 68,500
Henry donates shares to CRT worth		$100,000
CRT sells shares for		$100,000
CRT owes tax of		0
Amount left for CRT to reinvest		$100,000

In setting up his CRT, Henry has to make several decisions. First, he has to decide on the "income beneficiaries." He can choose himself, a friend, a relative, or virtually any combination. Then, he has to choose a payout period. The income can be paid over a fixed term, up to 20 years, or for the beneficiary's lifetime.

Henry chooses a lifetime income for himself and for his wife Ilene—probably the most common choice. Thus, both of them are guaranteed supplemental retirement income, no matter how long they live. After both deaths, the trust principal goes to their church.

FIXED OR VARIABLE?

Henry's next decisions relate to the income they'll receive. He can choose an "annuity trust" payout, meaning that he and Ilene will get a fixed sum, year after year. The minimum is 5 percent of the original trust principal, $5,000 in this example. Henry might choose to receive $5,000 a year, $6,000, $8,000, and so on. Once he makes that decision, the trust income is locked in for their lifetimes.

The other choice is a "unitrust" payout, a percentage of trust assets, again with a 5 percent minimum. Suppose Henry chooses a 6 percent unitrust. The first year, he and Ilene will receive $6,000—6 percent of $100,000.

If the trust earns more than 6 percent, the trust principal will increase and the 6 percent unitrust payout will be greater the second year. Conversely, if the trust earns less than the 6 percent payout, the second-year distribution will be smaller. And so on, through the life of the trust.

In essence, an annuity trust gives you a fixed income stream but leaves you vulnerable to inflation over the long-term. A unitrust gives you growth potential but exposes you to the risk of shrinking income if the trust funds aren't well-managed.

TABLE STAKES

What does this have to do with tax shelter? There are tables published by the IRS that you can use to calculate your tax deduction for transferring assets to a CRT. The IRS will let you deduct the "present value" of your future charitable contribution.

The smaller the amount you take each year as income, the greater the amount the charity can expect to receive down the line. And vice versa.

Similarly, in the case of lifetime income payments, the older the beneficiaries, the sooner the charities can expect to receive their share. The younger the beneficiaries, the longer the charities are likely to wait.

The IRS tables factor in life expectancies and trust payouts to come up with the amount you can deduct. The older the beneficiaries and the smaller the payout, the greater the tax deduction. The younger the beneficiaries and the greater the payout, the smaller the tax deduction.

Suppose Harry and Ilene, both in their late sixties, choose an 8 percent unitrust payout over their lifetimes. The IRS tables might show a 25 percent deduction. Therefore, by creating a $100,000 CRT, they get an immediate $25,000 charitable deduction. If they had stipulated a 9 percent or 10 percent unitrust payout, the upfront deduction would shrink.

WINNERS AND LOSERS

So the benefits to Henry and Ilene are clear. Instead of a $31,500 tax obligation, they get a $25,000 tax deduction. If their tax bracket is 35 percent, the $25,000 deduction cuts their tax bill by $8,750.

Plus, they get to enjoy the income from a $100,000 trust fund rather than $68,500 of after-tax sales proceeds.

In addition, they get the psychic satisfaction of knowing they will make a large contribution to their church after their deaths. In all likelihood, they'll get some recognition for their generosity from the church while they're still alive.

Of course, there's a catch. The stock funds they transfer to the CRT go to their church, not to their children. If Henry and Ilene had simply held onto the stock funds until their death, their kids would have inherited $100,000 worth of stock funds, plus any appreciation in the interim. (At the parents' death, the funds would have enjoyed the same stepped-up basis as described in Chapter 14, concerning real estate. Then, the kids could sell the shares and pay no tax on the capital gains.)

If Henry and Ilene had sold the stock funds and reinvested the after-tax proceeds in bond funds, living off the income, their kids would have inherited $68,500 worth of bond funds. Instead, they're shut out.

Now, that may be fine with Henry and Ilene. Their kids may have sufficient wealth in their own right, or they may be inheriting other assets. The stock funds are meant to go to charity.

In some cases, though, Henry and Ilene may want to compensate their children for their lost inheritance. They might use some of their tax savings or some of their increased income to buy a life insurance policy, payable to their children after their deaths. Often, the children's full inheritance can be preserved and the parents still will come out ahead: The only loser is the IRS.

CHARITABLE THOUGHTS

Insurance companies and brokerage firms often tout the virtues of CRTs. The former want to sell insurance policies to offset the lost inheritances; the latter want sales commissions and management fees for the money in the trust, which may be substantial. Often, the presentations promoting CRTs show you how everyone comes out way ahead.

That may or may not be the case: Insurers and brokers have few peers in massaging numbers. In truth, a CRT really is most suitable for you if you have a genuine charitable intent. After all, you're going to give away a large amount of valuable assets.

Nevertheless, many people do make sizable contributions over their lifetimes. You may, for example, want to support your alma mater. You may have a favorite cause you want to further: animal rights or aid to disabled veterans or cancer research, for example. Or, like Henry and Ilene, you may want to provide financial aid to a religious institution.

You can use a CRT to donate money to any of these. You'll know you "gave something back," and the charity may well honor you with recognition during your lifetime.

If you decide to establish a CRT for the benefit of a particular organization, contact the people there before you get too far along. The institution may pay the start-up costs if you agree to make your choice of a charitable beneficiary irrevocable. That's no small favor, because the up-front costs of a CRT may range from $1,500 to $2,500.

If you can't get someone else to pick up the tab, don't make your choice of charitable beneficiary irrevocable. You may start out with the intent of donating the proceeds to a local hospital, only to become disenchanted after a management change. If you've kept your options open, you can change the terms of the CRT, directing the money to be split between your alma mater and the Red Cross, for example.

(For this reason, and others, you're better off serving as trustee of the CRT yourself, or perhaps as co-trustee with a financial pro. As with any trust, the trustee is the one who makes all the decisions regarding the assets.)

NO TURNING BACK

Besides the expense, there are other drawbacks to setting up a CRT. A CRT must be irrevocable. Once you transfer assets, you can't reclaim them. (Although, as noted, you may be able to change charitable beneficiaries.)

There are some technical points to consider, so you must work with a knowledgeable lawyer. You shouldn't donate mortgaged property, for example, and hard-to-value assets should be appraised by an independent third party. That's true if you're contributing real estate or shares in a privately owned business.

From a tax viewpoint, the biggest hurdle is the annual limit on charitable deductions. Generally, when you donate long-term capital gains assets (for example, securities or real estate), you can't deduct more than 30 percent of your AGI in one year. Excess contributions can be "carried forward," deducted in the future, up to five years.

Henry and Ilene, for example, are entitled to a $25,000 deduction from their CRT. They'd need an AGI of at least $83,333 that year in order to get the full write-off. If their AGI is $50,000, for example, only $15,000 (30 percent of $50,000) could be deducted. The other $10,000 can be deducted next year, or the year after that.

This may not be a great problem for Henry and Ilene, but some people set up CRTs and contribute assets worth $500,000 or $1 million or more. They get deductions that run into six figures. In such cases, they need to plan carefully to make sure their deductions aren't wasted because they can't be taken within six years.

What can you do if you face a large charitable contribution and a relatively small AGI? One solution is to make a smaller contribution, one that you can deduct in full. After the deduction is used up, donate the rest of your assets, or another portion. If this is your strategy, you should choose a unitrust, where you can make additional contributions. You can't make second or third contributions to a CRT annuity trust.

PERSONAL PENSION PLAN

Here's a sophisticated variation on this shelter that can work if you want to increase your future retirement income or if you're a business owner looking for a retirement plan without the expense of standard plans. You can set up a CRT with a unitrust payout, including a provision that distributions can't exceed income. Then you, as trustee, can invest the trust proceeds in zero-coupon municipal bonds. (Zero-coupon bonds pay no interest until maturity.)

Drafted by a knowledgeable lawyer, such a trust will have no taxable income and won't have to make distributions. Because it's a unitrust, you can make annual contributions, if you wish, and the value of the zero-coupon municipals will grow, tax-free.

When you reach retirement age, you (as trustee) can sell the zero-coupon bonds and reinvest in taxable securities. Then the trust will have income and distributions can begin. If your trust included a "catch-up provision," the initial distributions can be greater to make up for the payments that were skipped.

Such CRTs have no limits on contributions and are not subject to the federal laws on qualified retirement plans. What's more, you'll get a partial tax deduction each time you make a contribution for the future charitable donation.

SUMMING UP

- If you have a large amount of appreciated assets, donating them to a charitable remainder trust can be a super tax shelter.

- The capital gains tax is avoided.
- You reduce your taxable estate without incurring gift or estate tax.
- You get an immediate charitable deduction even though the actual donation may be years away.
- After the CRT sells the appreciated assets, it can reinvest in income-producing assets and pay a lifetime income to you and a loved one.
- Besides the satisfaction of making a sizable contribution, you may get recognition from the charity that eventually will receive the trust assets.
- To make up for the inheritance lost to your heirs, you may buy insurance on your life, payable to them.
- A properly-structured CRT can be a means of saving for retirement, supplementing or replacing an IRA, Keogh, 401(k), or employer plan.

19 Child's Play
Shifting Income to Your Kids to Save Taxes

As any parent knows, kids are an expense. There seems to be no end to the bills for their food, their clothes, their schooling, their entertainment. The tax exemption you're allowed for each child—$2,350 in 1993, which will save you around $750 in tax—doesn't begin to cover the cost.

However, you may be able to find more tax shelter in your kids, by shifting some of your highly taxed income to their lower tax brackets. You probably are in a 28 percent or a 31 percent tax bracket, assuming your taxable income on a joint return is over $37,000 or so ($30,000 for a single taxpayer qualifying as a head of household). Various complexities of the tax code may push your real rate up a point or so. Under the Clinton Administration, tax brackets for high-income earners likely will hit 36 percent, even 40 percent. Moreover, most taxpayers need to pay state income taxes as well.

On the other hand, children may have a low bracket, even no bracket at all. A single taxpayer can earn around $22,000 and stay in the 15 percent tax bracket.

Your "tax bracket" is the rate you pay on your last dollar of income. Suppose, for example, Peg and Paul Perkins file a joint return, declaring $80,000 of taxable income. On December 15, their neighbor Betty Benson gives them a call. Betty is going away for a couple of weeks and would like to have some work done on the office she keeps in her home—walls painted, shelves installed, furniture moved, and so on. She'll pay $1,000 for the job.

Paul, who was planning to take some vacation time anyway, could do the job. However, in a 31 percent tax bracket, he'd owe $310 in tax and wind up with only $690. Instead, he suggests his son, Perry, do it while home from school. Perry, who reports about $5,000 a year from a part-time job, is in a 15 percent bracket. He'll owe only $150 on that extra $1,000 in income, so he gets to keep $850—$160 more than his parents would retain. When other taxes are figured in, the increase in net income may be even greater.

HIGH-POWERED SHIFTING

You can't count on jobs from neighbors in your tax planning. However, there are more predictable ways to shift income from parent to child and take advantage of low tax brackets.

For example, do you have taxable investment income? Interest from bank accounts or bonds, dividends from stocks or mutual funds? Unless that investment income is sheltered inside a retirement plan, the income will be added to all your other income and taxed at your highest rate. By putting the investments in your child's name, you can reduce your tax exposure.

Let's take the example of Joe and Mary Robinson, whose only investment income comes from a $100,000 CD. Assuming that CD earns 5 percent, that's $5,000 a year. In a 31 percent bracket, their tax obligation is $1,550 a year. If they put the CD in the name of their daughter, Diane, who's in a 15 percent bracket, she'll collect that same $5,000 and pay only $750 in tax. The Robinson family will be ahead by $800 a year.

Unfortunately, income shifting isn't that simple. There's a so-called "kiddie tax" structure that applies to children under 14. Here's how the kiddie tax works:

It applies to children under age 14 at the end of the taxable year. For 1994, for example, it applies to all children born in 1981 or later; for 1995, those born in 1982 or later, and so on. Those are the kiddies.

For children in that category, special rules apply to "unearned" or investment income. The first $600 a year is tax-free and the next $600 is taxed at only 15 percent. (Those numbers increase slightly each year.) Everything over $1,200 is taxed at the parent's or parents' rate.

Suppose, in our example, Diane Robinson is only 12 when she receives $5,000 a year from the $100,000 CD. Her tax obligation will be:

		Tax
First	$ 600	0
Next	$ 600 (@ 15 percent)	$ 90
Remaining	$3,800 (@ parents' 31 percent)	$1,178

As you can see, the tax shelter is limited to the first $1,200 a year. Therefore, if you have children under age 14, it pays for them to have up to $1,200 a year in investment income, but no more. The Robinsons, then, might move $24,000 into Diane's name. If she earns the same 5 percent interest, she'll receive $1,200 and owe only $90 in income tax—a blended tax rate of only 7.5 percent. The Robinsons will save $282 a year with this simple strategy.

FOR THE IRS, LIFE BEGINS AT 14

Once Diane turns age 14, the math changes. Again, the first $600 of investment income is tax-free, sheltered by her standard deduction. But now she can file as a regular single taxpayer, so up to $22,000 a year is taxed at only 15 percent.

Suppose, therefore, that the Robinsons gave Diane $24,000 worth of CDs before she turned 14. After she reaches age 14, they can give her the remaining $76,000. Now she'll get all $5,000 in interest, $600 tax free and $4,400 taxed at 15 percent. Therefore, after your child turns age 14, it pays to shift as much investment as possible, up to around $22,000 a year.

Other strategies can be used to take advantage of a child over age 14. Suppose, for example, you've been investing in EE Savings

Bonds to help finance your child's college education. Further suppose that your income is over the limits mentioned in Chapter 9, so the interest will be taxable. You can transfer the bonds to your child, who can redeem them. The interest will be taxable at your child's 15 percent rate.

This ploy is by no means limited to EE Savings Bonds. Ted and Linda Walker, for example, have been investing regularly in mutual funds ever since their son Sam was born. Now it's time for Sam to go to college and the Walkers want to cash in their bonds. Thanks to the strong stock market over the past 17 years, they have large profits on their mutual funds. If they sold them, they'd owe tax at 28 percent.

They sell mutual funds worth	$20,000
Their basis in the fund shares is	$ 8,000
They'd have a taxable gain of	$12,000
At a 28 percent rate, they'd owe	$ 3,360

Instead, they transfer the $20,000 in fund shares to Sam, who sells them. The gain is the same—$12,000—but now it's Sam's gain, taxed at only 15 percent. He pays $1,800 in tax and the family saves $1,560, simply by shifting their mutual fund shares to Sam.

If you're about to sell assets at a capital gain, and you have a child age 14 or over, always think about a transfer to your child before the sale.

Note what happens if you have two or three children aged 14+. Each one has a 15 percent tax bracket up to about $22,000 a year. Thus, if you have larger gains to cash in, you could split your transfers among your children. You could cut your tax on $44,000, even $66,000 worth of gains a year.

If you have even larger gains, split the gifts by year. Give some assets for sale in December, some assets for sale the following January, for example.

GENEROSITY HAS ITS LIMITS

There's another tax to consider when you start transferring assets to your children: the gift tax. This tax, unified with the estate tax, is covered in Chapter 23. The essence is that you can run up a huge tax bill, now or in the future, if you're careless in giving gifts.

Under current law, $10,000 is the magic number. Anybody can give up to $10,000 worth of assets each year to an unlimited number of recipients. There are no gift tax consequences, not even a gift tax return to fill out.

John Davis, for example, has three children. He can give each of them $10,000 in 1994 without running into the gift tax. He can give each another $10,000 in 1995, and so on. He can give cash or stocks, bonds, mutual fund shares, and so forth. If he gives away something that's harder to value, he'll probably need an independent appraisal.

Suppose John is married to Carol. She, too, can give away up to $10,000 a year to each of their three children. If it's not convenient for both spouses to give $10,000 gifts, one can give away $20,000 per year per recipient, as long as the other spouse approves of the gift.

If you're shifting income-producing or appreciated assets to your children to take advantage of their low tax bracket, try to live within the $10,000 or $20,000 limits. Larger gifts are possible but they require the advice of a tax pro. In essence, when you make gifts that exceed the $10,000 or $20,000 limit, you may be reducing your family's shelter from estate taxes.

WORK-FARE

There's another way to take advantage of your children's low rates, one that doesn't involve the kiddie tax or the gift tax. However, this shelter is available only for business owners, professionals, the self-employed, or those who participate in a sideline business.

What's the shelter? Hire your own kids.

Here, the money you pay your kids will be deductible for you or for your business. Your kids will owe little or no tax on the money they receive.

For example, Dr. Jill Harris is solidly in the 31 percent tax bracket. She has a clerk-receptionist, but the paperwork generated by her pediatrics practice seems never-ending. Therefore, she pays her two children to come in and help, weekends and school holidays.

Over the course of the year, she pays her children a total of $4,000. She deducts that $4,000, saving herself $1,240: her $4,000 deduction times her 31 percent bracket.

How is that $4,000 taxed? Not at all. For earned income, all workers—even dependents—are entitled to a standard deduction up to $3,700 in 1993, increasing in subsequent years. Because her two children earn $2,200 and $1,800, respectively, they're well under the limit. They owe no tax at all, and the Harris family is ahead by $1,240.

Dr. Jill could pay her kids even more, increasing her tax shelter. Even if they exceeded the $3,700 limit, they'd be in a 15 percent bracket, so the Harris family would still be winners because Jill is taking deductions at 31 percent. What's more, the kids can contribute up to $2,000 apiece into an IRA, escaping even the 15 percent tax.

You don't have to be a doctor to use this shelter. As long as you're in a position to hire someone and deduct the payments, you can cut your tax burden this way while keeping money in the family.

There are other advantages to this strategy, too. Your kids can get some spending money, put funds aside for college, or both. They'll get to know something about your business. Perhaps most important, they'll get to learn what it's like to work for pay.

Although this is an excellent tax shelter, you can't abuse it. Your kids must actually do the work for which they're paid, and you can't overpay them. If you hire your 10-year-old to do some filing, clean up your office, run errands, and so forth, you might justify paying $5 an hour, not $25. Keep a record showing that the work really was done and treat your kids as you would any other employees.

NO STRINGS

Whether you transfer investment assets to your children, pay them for working, or both, one question has to be solved: How will your kids hold their money? As long as your kids are minors (under age 18 or 21, depending on the state), they're not legally able to make decisions about their money, so they'll need some sort of special account.

In most cases, your kids' money can be held in a custodial account. Depending upon your state, these accounts are established under the Uniform Gifts to Minors Act (UGMA) or the Uniform Transfers to Minors Act (UTMA).

UGMA and UTMA accounts are easy to establish, usually with no fee. You, as parent, can act as custodian. Thus, if you want to transfer securities to your children, you can move them into a custodial account, with you as custodian, so you can continue to make decisions. You can sell the securities when you want to.

Is there a tax trap with a custodial account? You can't use funds from the account to pay ordinary parental expenses. If so, the IRS may say that the account really belongs to you and tax you on the account's income. You can use the account to fund extraordinary expenses—scuba camp or a trip to Europe—but not for everyday maintenance.

A greater concern, for more people, is that transfers to a custodial account belong to your children. You can't put the money back into your pocket when it suits you. Then, when your children become "emancipated," as the expression goes, or come of age (18 or 21), whatever is in the account belongs to them, no strings attached. There's no way you can force your kids to use the money for college, for example.

So you have to use some common sense when you make transfers to your kids. Don't give away money you'll need for your own living expenses, your own retirement. Once you give the money to your kids, it's theirs. The best solution is for that money to be used to pay for college and perhaps give them a start on going off to live independently.

(Yet another complicating factor affecting gifts to minors is college aid. According to the standard formulas, a family's expected contribution goes up as money is shifted from parents to kids. So if you're expecting substantial financial aid in sending your children to college—you have few assets and a low income—don't shift assets. However, if you're not realistically expecting much in the way of financial aid, the tax savings can make it easier for you to pay for college.)

A MATTER OF TRUST

If you're planning on transferring large amounts of money to your children, another option is a trust, which can be drawn up to last until your kids are 25, 30, and so on, ensuring that the money will be used for education instead of squandered. Moreover, setting up the trust introduces another taxpayer into the picture—the trust itself. By keeping some income inside the trust and paying some out to your children (for college expenses), you can keep more income in low tax brackets.

Don't rush into a trust for your children. In most cases, you can wait until they're 15 or 16. By then, you'll be able to judge whether or not they're responsible. If you think there's a good chance they'll put their money into a sports car instead of into college tuition, you'll still have time to create a trust on their behalf.

SHIFT DEDUCTIONS THE OTHER WAY

The ability to use your kids as a tax shelter doesn't end when they become adults. You still can make gifts to them, shifting investment income from your high bracket to their low bracket. Another valuable strategy is to buy a house for your kids (see Chapter 13), effectively shifting deductions from their low bracket to your high bracket.

Deduction shifting can go the other way, too. Suppose Malcolm Lewis' widowed mother Rose lives comfortably on social security, a pension, and investment income. She pays income tax in the 15 percent bracket.

In her low bracket, it makes little tax sense for Rose to own the condo in which she lives. The mortgage interest and property tax deductions are not worth much to her. If Malcolm and his wife, Marjorie, own the condo and rent it to Rose, they can take those deductions at their tax rate, more than 40 cents on the dollar. Rose can pay rent to her son and daughter-in-law, who'll take depreciation deductions in their high bracket. The more deductions that can be shifted from a 15 percent bracket to 40 percent, the more tax shelter the Lewis family will enjoy.

SUMMING UP

- The higher your tax bracket, the more it pays to shift income to low-bracket children.
- Children under age 14 should have up to $1,200 worth of taxable investment income per year, but no more.
- Children 14 or older can have as much as $22,000 in income and pay tax at a low 15 percent.
- Before you sell appreciated assets, give them to children (subject to gift tax limitations) and have the children sell those assets in 15 percent bracket.
- If you're in a position to hire your kids, you'll take deductions in your high bracket while your kids owe little or no tax.
- Hiring your kids has many virtues but you have to pay them a reasonable amount for work they actually perform.
- Money your kids earn or receive can be held in a custodial account.
- If you're concerned that your kids will squander their money after they come of age, you can use a trust to preserve the assets.
- When your kids first become independent, with relatively low earnings, they'll receive little benefit from tax deductions, so it may make sense for you to buy a house and rent to them.
- Similarly, there may be tax savings if you buy a house or condo that you rent to low-bracket elderly parents.

20 Defer and Conquer
Year-End Tax-Planning Strategies

It's always better to pay later rather than sooner. That's especially true with taxes, for two reasons.

First, there's the time value of money. Say you have a tax obligation of $10,000 for 1994, payable in April 1995. By some skillful planning, you defer $1,000 of that tax to 1995, payable in 1996.

Now you have the use of that $1,000 for an extra year. That's worth $50 to you, if you earn 5 percent on that money; $100 if you can earn 10 percent. The more you can defer and the higher your earnings, the more valuable the tax deferral.

Plus, deferring tax gives you another year to plan. Between April 1995 and April 1996, you may be able to come up with some way of sheltering that deferred $1,000 in tax.

Sometimes, you'll see articles advising you to accelerate tax payments because tax rates are expected to rise in the next year. Generally, that doesn't make sense. No one really knows what tax legislation will look like until it's passed, so why go out of your way to speed payments to the IRS? You're better off with the bird-in-the-hand of tax deferral. Therefore, proven ways to accelerate deductions into this year and delay income until next year are effective tax shelters.

A 15-MONTH GAIN, NO PAIN

If you have a substantial amount in a money market fund or a day-to-day bank account, money you probably won't need right away, switch into Treasury bills or CDs. You can get 15 months of tax deferral that way.

Treasury bills are short-term obligations of the federal government, with maturities of 90 days, 180 days, or one year. The minimum purchase is $10,000.

Actually, that's not true. You buy T-bills at a discount, paying $9,700 or $9,800 or $9,912 or whatever is the current offering price. At maturity, you get your $10,000. That's when the income tax is due.

For example, you buy a 180-day T-bill in July 1994 for $9,800. In January 1995, the T-bill matures and you get your $10,000, including the $200 interest, which you put into your pocket.

That $200 is considered taxable income in 1995. You don't have to pay tax on it until you file your 1995 tax return, probably in April 1996. (If you make quarterly estimated tax payments, taxes will be due sooner.) Because a T-bill is a Treasury security, interest is exempt from state and local income taxes, so there's a good bit of shelter, along with the absolute safety of T-bills.

By contrast, if you had just left the $9,800 in a money market fund, the interest earned would have been immediately taxable.

Therefore, if you want to defer tax on investment income, you can buy a T-bill that will mature in January, February, or March of the following year. When that matures, if there's still no pressing need for ready cash, you can use the proceeds to buy a one-year T-bill, deferring tax on a full year's worth of income.

The same strategy works for CDs, too, as long as you ask the bank to credit the interest at maturity. There's no exemption from state or local income tax with a CD, but you can invest smaller amounts than the $10,000 needed for a T-bill.

WRITE OUT THE OLD YEAR...

Each December, be sure to write certain checks so you lock in a deduction for the current year:

- Pay your state and local income taxes early. If you file quarterly estimated tax returns, your last 1994 payment, for example, is due in January 1995. Make the payment a couple of weeks early, in December 1994, and you'll get the deduction in 1994 rather than in 1995.

  Even if you don't make estimated tax payments, you may owe state or local income tax if your withholding throughout the year won't cover your obligation. (You may, for example, have taxable investment income.) In this case, make the payment in December 1994, to get a 1994 tax deduction, rather than wait until April 1995.

- Pay your property taxes early. If you're a homeowner, you may get a property tax bill calling for payments, say, in August, November, February, and May. In this case, you can make your February and May payments in December, to accelerate the deduction.

- Make your January mortgage payment early. Make sure your lender receives it well before December 31.

- Make whatever charitable contributions you can. If necessary, charge them on credit cards for later payment. As long as the charge is made in December, you can take a deduction for that year.

BUNCH TIME

Many itemized deductions are tied to your adjusted gross income (AGI). Medical costs are deductible only if they're over 7.5 percent of AGI; miscellaneous costs (for example, tax-preparation fees, unreimbursed employee business expenses) only if they're over 2 percent of AGI; casualty losses only if they're over 10 percent. It's better to bunch expenses to get deductions every other year, for example, rather than lose the deductions, year after year.

Your first step is to estimate your AGI for the current year. Start with last year's tax return—your AGI is the last number on the bottom of the first side of Form 1040. Then make the appropriate adjustment, based on whether you think this year's AGI will be greater or lower.

For example, Fred and Flo Morris had a $45,000 AGI in 1993. They estimate 1994 AGI a bit higher, around $50,000. They can deduct medical costs that exceed 7.5 percent of their AGI, or $3,750. That is, if their total medical costs are $6,000, they can deduct $2,250.

In December 1994, Fred and Flo add up their medical expenses for the year so far, including health insurance premiums, doctor and hospital bills, and so on. They discover they've already spent $4,000. Thus, every additional dollar they spend on medical expenses in 1994 will be deductible.

Therefore, Fred buys that expensive new pair of bifocals his eye doctor has been urging him to get; Flo has the root canal work she's been putting off. When the bill for their next health insurance premium comes in, they make sure to pay it before December 31.

On the other hand, suppose Fred and Flo have spent only $2,000 in 1994 medical expenses. They're a long way from the threshold, so they defer all their medical expenses to 1995, when they might be deductible, if medical costs increase.

You need to go through a similar exercise with miscellaneous expenses and casualty losses, with 2 percent and 10 percent thresholds, respectively.

There's a special circumstance with medical and casualty deductions: Often, you'll be reimbursed by insurance, which will offset your deductions.

If your expenses are incurred late in the year, you may want to wait until the following year to file the insurance claims. Thus, you'll get an immediate deduction, provided you're over the threshold, while deferring the taxable income to the following year.

A CAPITAL IDEA

Investors can use other year-end tax shelters. Perhaps most important, try to adjust your portfolio so you wind up each year with a $3,000 net capital loss. You can deduct this amount from your otherwise taxable income. Net capital losses over $3,000 per year have to be carried forward to future years.

For example, in December 1994, Paul checks over his brokerage statements for the year and finds he has sold two stocks at a total gain of $10,000, transferred out of some mutual funds for a total loss of $5,000. Thus, he has a $5,000 net capital gain for the year. So far.

He looks over his entire portfolio to see if he can take some losses. He discovers that his corporate bonds are sharply off in price because interest rates have risen. So he tells his broker to sell enough bonds to generate an $8,000 loss. This gives him a $3,000 net capital loss for 1994, which he can deduct, rather than a $5,000 gain, on which he'd owe taxes.

Of course, Paul now has cash rather than the bonds, which he sold. If he sold AT&T bonds, for example, he can use the money to buy GE bonds or Exxon bonds or some other high-grade corporate bonds. His portfolio, then, remains essentially unchanged while he's saved around $2,500 in taxes.

What if Paul insists on AT&T bonds in his portfolio? He has to wait 31 days before buying back the AT&T bonds, taking the risk that prices will rise in the interim. If he doesn't wait that long, the IRS will disallow any loss on the first sale of the bonds.

Once you've lined up a $3,000 capital loss for the year, back off. Defer selling your house or other capital gain property until the following year.

BOXED IN

In some years, you'll come to December holding stocks that have appreciated sharply and that you'd like to sell. Perhaps you're afraid of a market correction. However, if you sell the shares in December 1994, you'll have a large tax obligation in 1994, payable by April 1995.

In this case, you can use a strategy known as a "short sale against the box." Although this sounds complicated, it really isn't. Instead of selling 100 shares of Wal-Mart at a $100 price, to take your profits, you ask your broker to let you borrow another 100 shares of Wal-Mart, using your first 100 shares as collateral. Then you sell short the borrowed shares (that is, promise to sell them) at the $100 market price.

Now you've locked in your profit. If Wal-Mart's price falls, you'll gain on the short position what you lose on your original stock position. And vice versa, if Wal-Mart stock goes up above $100.

In January, you can use your original shares to close out your short position. Assuming a modest move in the interim, you'll have a net gain from your original investment in Wal-Mart. Now, though, you'll have all of 1995 to plan around your capital gain on Wal-Mart.

TURN DECEMBER INCOME INTO JANUARY INCOME

Do you have some leeway in timing your income? Maybe you're self-employed or you run a part-time sideline business out of your home. If that's the case, don't send out invoices in late November-early December. Wait until it's too late in the year for your customers to receive your bills and pay you.

As a result, you'll get your money in January rather than in December. By deferring your income for a month, you'll defer your tax for a year.

By the same token, it pays to accelerate expenses related to self-employment income or a sideline business. Check over your stationery supplies in December and buy a year's worth of business cards, typing paper, computer diskettes, and the like. If you're going to buy some equipment, anything ranging from a briefcase to a desktop publishing system, do it in December. Again, you can charge it on a credit card if you want to defer the actual payment.

If you have self-employment income but not a Keogh plan, set one up before December 31. You don't have to contribute funds until you file your tax return.

Employees, too, may be able to do some income-shifting: If you expect a year-end bonus, ask your employer if you can receive it in January rather than in December.

Year-end is the time when most employees have to make decisions about 401(k) plans and flexible spending accounts, so make sure you fund them as fully as you can. (If you're already in an FSA, be sure to spend the entire amount before year-end because there are no refunds or rollovers.)

THE JOY OF GIVING

If you're planning to reduce estate tax (see Chapter 23), be sure to make tax-free gifts. Under current law, you can give away up to $10,000 worth of assets per year to any number of recipients, free of gift tax. If your spouse consents, you can give away up to $20,000 per year. Such gifts are "use-it-or-lose-it." If you don't make gifts in 1994, for example, you can't double up in 1995.

SUMMING UP

- Deferring income and accelerating deductions can reduce your tax for the current year and give you time to plan around the deferred obligation.
- If you have excess funds in day-to-day bank accounts or money market funds, shift into T-bills or CDs maturing the following year.
- Pay outstanding state and local tax obligations before the year is up.
- If your annual medical expenses are over 7.5 percent of your adjusted gross income for the year, make elective medical payments by year-end.
- Sell securities at year-end, for gains or losses, so that you wind up with a $3,000 net capital loss each year.
- If you have an appreciated stock you'd like to sell at year-end, a short sale against the box can lock in the gain while deferring the tax.
- If you're self-employed, schedule your billing so you don't receive December payments.
- Employees should request that bonuses be deferred until January.
- If you're concerned about estate tax, be sure to make your annual gifts of up to $10,000 per recipient each year.

21 Taking the Sting out of State and Local Levies

Finding Shelter from Other Taxmen

So far, this book has been mainly concerned about federal taxes. Unfortunately, the IRS is not the only tax collector from whom you need shelter. State and local taxes take an increasingly painful bite.

The best way to cut state and local income taxes? Reduce your federal income tax. Most states peg their tax collection to Uncle Sam, one way or another. Many of the shelters already described will do double or even triple duty.

Other special shelters have already been mentioned. Locally issued municipal bonds, for example, generally escape all income taxes. U.S. Treasury securities, including EE Savings Bonds, pay interest that's exempt from state and local income tax, although they're subject to federal tax. Investors in high-tax states and cities should emphasize local munis and Treasuries and mutual funds that hold them. For safety, stick with short- and medium-term issues.

WHEN TAXES HIT HOME

Of all the taxes that you pay, the property tax on your home may be the most arbitrary. Typically, the tax rate is set by law, in your community, then applied to your property "value," to get the amount due. Suppose your local rate is 4 percent and your house is assessed at $100,000: Your property tax bill will be $4,000 per year.

The weak link here is the valuation. There is no way to know for sure what your home really is worth until you sell it, at which point you'll no longer owe the property taxes. What's more, a house worth $100,000 one year may be worth $90,000 or $110,000 the next year, depending on market conditions.

Most communities rely on periodic appraisals to set values for property tax purposes. Appraising real estate is more art than science. If you can demonstrate that your home has been overvalued, you can reduce your property tax. What's more, that lower tax carries over to future years.

For example, you convince your township that your house really is worth $90,000, not $100,000. At a 4 percent rate, your property tax drops to $3,600 per year, from $4,000. You'll save that $400 every year until the next appraisal.

Mistakes in property appraisals are made more often than not. Orange County, Florida (including Orlando), has 39 appraisers to cover 270,000 real estate parcels. Hibbing, Minnesota, has just two assessors for 10,000 properties. The same situation applies in most cities and towns, so there's no way each property can be evaluated accurately. Therefore, it's entirely likely you'll find errors if you take the trouble to look.

ASSESSMENT ADJUSTMENT

Procedures for appealing tax assessments vary from community to community, but the basic approach is similar in most areas. First, find out where the records are kept, probably at your local assessor's office. Then ask to see the current record on your property.

This record will contain a listing with the size of your property, materials used, and other features that affect value. If there's a factual error (for example, the recorded size is much larger than the actual size), you generally can have the record corrected and your tax bill correspondingly reduced without going through a formal appeal.

When Karen M., a Washington, D.C., policy analyst, saw her tax bill rise 120 percent in one year, she found that a clerk had put the wrong lot number on her card, so she was being taxed as if she owned the larger condo next door. She corrected the error and got a $500 (almost 30 percent) tax reduction. Another homeowner saved $1,200 a year by proving that his house had a partial second story rather than a full one, as recorded. Unfortunately, he'd already paid the excess for 28 years, and no refund was offered.

Even without a factual error, you might be able to convince your assessor to drop your valuations. Retired teacher Carol T., of Palatine, Illinois, got a jolt when she was hit with a 61 percent property tax increase one year, from $1,212 to $1,956. She went to the assessor's office with photos showing flood damage that rainwater runoff from a neighbor's property regularly inflicts upon her yard. The assessor cut her tax increase to 31 percent right there, saving her $372 a year.

TAX APPEAL

In some cases, you will have to file an appeal by filling out an application. Before you appeal, try to get these facts from the assessor's office:

- *Your neighbors' assessments.* Find out if your home is valued at a higher figure than comparable houses in your vicinity. Get the assessments of at least three (preferably five) properties that are comparable to yours. You might even go as far as Richard E. of Sarasota, Florida, who made up a list of 16 properties on a two-block stretch of his street. He pointed out, among other inconsistencies, that a six-bedroom house built in 1961 was assessed at $43,622 while his four-bedroom house built in 1953 was assessed at $51,250. Because he made his case so strongly, his assessment was dropped by $9,700, reducing his annual tax bill by $225.

- *Recent sales prices.* If you can show that recent sales of comparable homes have been in the $75,000 to $90,000 price range, for example, you may be able to reduce a $100,000 valuation. John C., a real estate developer in Verona, New Jersey, bought a condo in a complex he had helped to build. The condo was valued at $200,000, the price such units commanded at the 1987 market peak. But John hired a lawyer who showed recent prices to be in the $160,000 area. The matter was settled out of court, with a valuation reduced to $167,446, and John won a three-year tax reduction of $2,499.

- *Price/value ratios.* Often, homes are not assessed at full value for tax purposes. By comparing the assessed values of homes recently sold to their selling prices, you can see how yours compares.

    For example, the 10 most recent sales of homes comparable to yours averaged $150,000. The assessments on those homes averaged $90,000. Therefore, the average assessed value is 60 percent of the selling price.

    If you bought your home for $125,000, and it's assessed at $100,000, that's an 80 percent ratio. Backed up by these numbers, you might get a reduced assessment on your house.

LOOK BEFORE LEAPING

Before you prepare your appeal, make sure it's filed on time. Sometimes there will be a deadline printed on the assessment notice.

According to the National Taxpayers Union, you should attend someone else's appeals hearing before you go in for your own. You'll see what the procedures are and what kinds of questions you're likely to be asked.

At your hearing, be sure you have copies of all your assessment records. If your home is in need of repair, bring in professional estimates as to what those repairs will cost. Bring photos to make your points. For a brochure on "How to Fight Property Taxes," send

$2 to the National Taxpayers Union, 325 Pennsylvania Ave., S.E., Washington, DC 20003.

Once you get to know the assessment routine, you can antici-pate the taxman. Tom K., an attorney working for the federal gov-ernment, won one battle with the Washington, D.C., assessor's office. Two years later, aware that his home would be revalued, he invited the assessor in for a visit. After seeing the water-stained living room ceiling, raw plaster in the upstairs hallway, and an incomplete bath-room renovation, the valuation was actually reduced by $30,000, knocking down the tax bill by $288 a year.

HIRED GUNS

If you'd rather not handle the paper chase yourself, or if you're not confident you'll do it right, you can hire a consultant to appeal your assessment. Ask your accountant, attorney, or Realtor for recommen-dations. Generally, a consultant will take little or no money up front, charging you 20 percent to 50 percent of your first-year tax savings as a fee. Before you hire a consultant, though, ask employees in your local assessor's office—often, they're willing to help you through the paperwork.

The same procedures for appealing property tax on your home apply to investment property as well. The higher your property tax, the greater the payoff from even a small reduction in assessed value.

According to press reports, over half of all homeowners who appeal their property tax succeed. Their savings might be a few hundred or a few thousand dollars. More than that, those savings will be enjoyed each year, while you have a lower base for ongoing property tax increases.

Plus, the lower your property taxes, the greater your home's resale value.

SUNSET STRIP

After a career as an unemployment insurance supervisor for the state of California, Gertrude E. moved to Nevada, where she lived mod-estly on a fixed income of $12,000 a year. Imagine her surprise, 10 years later, when she got a bill from California for 10 years of back taxes, interest, and a 55 percent penalty. The total tab: $8,000!

Gertrude was not alone. California collects over $10 million a year from retirees who no longer live there. Other states, notably New York, Oregon, Minnesota, Vermont, Arkansas, Kansas, Iowa, and Michigan also reach out for retirees, and the list is sure to grow.

You may wonder, why should Gertrude or anyone else pay tax to a state where you no longer live and from which you no longer receive any services? Well, here's how the states see it:

You worked in California or New York or wherever, incurring an income tax obligation. Some of those taxes, though, were not paid because of contributions to pension plans or IRAs or Keoghs. Now you've moved to Florida or Nevada or some other low-tax state and you're taking money out of your retirement funds. Well, your old state wants the deferred taxes. Thanks to modern computers linked to one another, states can track down retirees. To enforce its demands for retiree taxes, states may place liens on property left there; they may even send in bill collectors to your new home.

How can you avoid this late hit? One solution is to move to Nevada and take all your assets with you. In 1989, after hearing complaints from Gertrude E. and many others like her, the state passed a law preventing other states from attaching property or bank accounts of Nevada retirees to pay back-tax bills. Now Gertrude E. no longer pays her $50 a month to California.

If Nevada isn't the end of your rainbow, meet with a local tax pro before you move. Your state may have a shelter you can use. New York, for example, doesn't tax pension annuities, so you could arrange to take your retirement money in monthly installments. Maryland doesn't apply its 7.5 percent state and local income tax to nonresident pension income, so one executive moved to Florida before receiving a large lump sum, saving nearly $500,000.

Some states tax employer pensions but not IRAs. The solution: Roll over pension funds into an IRA before making withdrawals.

As another solution, you may be able to contest your former state's tax assessment by showing that you lived in some other state while you worked and made retirement plan contributions. Or demonstrate that the buildup largely occurred after you left your old state. The better your records and the better your tax adviser, the more chance you'll have of slipping out of your old state's clutches.

If you wind up paying some tax to your old state, be sure to claim a credit: In most cases, this will reduce the income tax you'll owe to your new state. If you pay taxes on your pension plan to New Jersey, for example, the amount you pay generally would be deducted from what you'd owe to New York.

ONE STATE AT A TIME

More than anything else, once you move, move. Do everything you can to establish "domicile" in your new state. Otherwise, both states may claim you as a resident and you'll face two demands for income taxes while you're alive and for estate tax after your death.

Here are some steps you can take to establish domicile:

- Spend more than half the year in your new state.
- Join a local church or synagogue.
- Participate in local government bodies, civic and charitable organizations.
- Open local bank and brokerage accounts.
- Change your voting registration.
- Execute a new will.
- Change your auto insurance and registration.
- Obtain a burial plot.
- Change addresses on all legal documents, passports, and subscriptions.
- Sell all property and discontinue all memberships in your old state.
- Inform your old state that you have a new domicile.

If you're challenged, it's up to you to prove domicile, so make your case as strong as possible.

SUMMING UP

- Property taxes are based on a valuation of your home, and such valuations are usually inexact.
- If you can show that your valuation is too high or that a factual error has been made, you can get your property tax bill reduced.
- To justify a lower value, find out how your home is assessed compared to similar homes.
- Study the appeals process before making your own presentation.
- You can hire a consultant to reduce your assessment, paying a percentage of your initial tax savings.
- If you move from one state to another in retirement, your old state may try to tax the income from your IRA, Keogh, and corporate retirement plans.
- Discuss strategies with your tax pro before you move.
- Your best bet may be to show you built up your retirement nest egg while you were working elsewhere, not in the state attempting to collect tax.
- If you pay tax to more than one state, claim offsetting credits to reduce your total tax bill.
- When you move, take all steps necessary to establish domicile in your new state.

22 Death Without Taxes

Protect Your Family by Minimizing Estate Tax

Tax shelter isn't just about avoiding income tax. There's another tax worth escaping: the unified federal gift and estate tax. Using audit-proof shelters for this tax won't benefit you personally, but it will save your family many thousands of dollars.

In some ways, the estate tax is even crueler than the income tax. For one, it's a tax on money that's already been taxed. All your life, you work and pay income tax on your earnings. Whatever is left, you invest, and probably pay tax on those earnings. Finally, whatever you wind up with may be taxed yet again.

What's more, estate tax rates are higher than income tax rates. The federal income tax rate doesn't exceed 40 percent while estates are taxed as high as 55 percent.

Finally, the estate tax can demand a huge chunk of cash from your family on money you've never seen. Take the case of Larry Mason, who worked for years to build up a plumbing-supply business. The business was profitable, enabling Larry to enjoy a comfortable but by no means opulent lifestyle.

Larry, who was divorced, died and left his entire estate to his children. Virtually all of his assets consisted of his home, his plumbing business, and some real estate (an office building, a warehouse) he owned in connection with that business.

The way Larry's estate was valued, those assets were worth $2 million and his estate owed about $600,000 in federal estate tax. However, Larry left virtually no cash, and his children had nowhere near $600,000. Yet they had to raise the cash within nine months, so assets had to be sold in a hurry, at distress prices, to pay the estate tax.

THE REAL BOTTOM LINE

Through the 1980s and the early 1990s, up to this writing, the federal estate tax affected only those few estates that might be considered "rich," by some standards. However, the federal budget deficit has grown so huge that some increase in the gift and estate tax is likely. If you have any assets at all—a house, cars, insurance policy—you should know how the estate tax works and what steps you should take to ease its bite.

After you die, an executor you have nominated (or one a court has appointed) will handle your affairs and distribute your assets. One of your executor's responsibilities is to be sure that an estate tax return is filed within nine months.

On this return, your executor must put a value on all of your assets. That will include your home, your investment portfolio, your retirement fund. If you owned an antique shotgun collection, that needs to be valued. If you had a one-third interest in a partnership that owns an apartment building, the building must be valued and one-third of that amount must be included. And so on, including your jewelry and home furnishings and cash in the bank.

Your executor adds up all these assets, subtracts your debts, and finds your net worth. On that amount, estate tax is due.

Before your estate has to pay the tax, though, you're allowed some relief. For one, any assets that you leave to a spouse will be untaxed. You could die with a $25 million estate, leave everything to your spouse, and no estate tax would be due.

In addition, every estate gets a tax credit for up to $600,000 worth of assets. That is, if you die with an estate of $500,000, no estate tax would be due. If you die with $700,000, the first $600,000 would be exempt and $100,000 would be subject to tax. (The tax rate at this level is 37 percent, so your estate would owe $37,000.)

There has been wide speculation that the $600,000 threshold will be reduced, perhaps to $400,000 or $300,000. If so, the numbers will change, but the tax shelter strategies will remain the same.

USE IT OR LOSE IT

To see how *not* to reduce estate tax, consider the case of John and Mary Simpson, who have a gross estate of $1 million. John dies first and leaves everything to Mary. A year later, Mary dies and leaves everything to their children. Of her $1 million estate, $400,000 is subject to estate tax, so their children owe about $150,000.

With a little planning, the Simpsons could have saved $150,000 in taxes! John and Mary could have divided their estate so that each held $500,000 in assets. On John's death, his $500,000 goes directly to their children. Because it's below the $600,000 threshold, no estate tax is due.

Then, when Mary dies, her $500,000 goes to the children. Again, no estate tax is due. The Simpsons pass $1 million to their children with zero estate tax.

How did they save $150,000? By using John's estate tax shelter. In the previous example, where everything was left to Mary, John's shelter wasn't used. Mary was left with too much to shelter.

As long as the estate tax exemption stays at $600,000, a married couple can shelter up to $1.2 million from estate tax. At each parent's death, $600,000 will be passed on to the children, tax-free, for a total of $1.2 million.

If the exemption falls to, say, $400,000, the total a couple can shelter falls to $800,000. Nevertheless, good planning is necessary to save hundreds of thousands in taxes.

EVEN'S BETTER

This shelter obviously works best if the assets are divided 50–50: John has $500,000, Mary has $500,000. But what if John has $800,000 in assets in his name while Mary has only $200,000?

John can give Mary $300,000. For spousal gifts, there are no tax consequences. Now, the estates will be equalized.

Suppose John doesn't want to give $300,000 to Mary. He can leave up to $600,000 to the children, with the balance going to Mary. Again, no estate tax will be due.

Unless Mary dies first. Even if she leaves all of her $200,000 to the children, John's estate will be over $600,000, in taxable territory. That's the price they have to pay if they're unwilling to equalize estates.

Jointly owned property may be another problem. Such property automatically goes to the co-owner; it can't be left to someone else to use the estate tax exemption. Therefore, although joint ownership may offer comfort to some people, it often interferes with good tax planning. If your prime goal is to find shelter from estate tax, try to hold your property in one spouse's name.

SPOUSE CARE

Even if all property is held singly and the estates are equalized, there's another flaw with the preceding scenario. John dies first and leaves $500,000 to the children. That leaves Mary with $500,000 worth of assets. Mary may not have enough to live comfortably, especially if her assets are largely illiquid (for example, the family home) and if yields on savings accounts are low.

Here's the usual solution: Instead of leaving $500,000 outright to the children, John leaves $500,000 to a trust. This trust, often called a "credit shelter" trust or a "by-pass" trust, might provide for a lifetime income to Mary. In case of emergency, the trustee can tap the principal on Mary's behalf. At her death, the assets go to the children. Such a trust can be set up so it won't qualify for the unlimited marital deduction, so it will be sheltered by the $600,000 exemption.

Now, Mary has the full use of the $1 million estate for as long as she lives. At her death, all the money can pass to the children, free of estate tax.

One common technique is for John and Mary to state, in their wills, that such a trust will be established, at the first spouse's death, funded up to the amount of the estate tax exemption. Then, no matter what the exemption is, you'll be able to take full advantage.

If you have a larger estate, the same principle applies. Each spouse should have at least $600,000 worth of assets in his or her name. At the first death, a trust will be created, funded up to the amount of the estate tax exemption, permitted under current law.

DIS-COMFORT

Remember, the point of all this is to leave up to $600,000 to the next generation, not the surviving spouse, to take advantage of the $600,000 estate tax shelter. If the $600,000 in trust really is left to the surviving spouse, it will be subject to estate tax at her death, and the shelter is wasted.

Therefore, you have to be very careful in the wording of the trust. It's all right, the IRS has ruled, for the trustee to be able to give money to the spouse for "maintenance, education, support, or health." That doesn't mean the trust fund belongs to her.

However, as *Forbes* has reported, many lawyers add language providing that the survivor has access to the trust funds for her "comfort" or "enjoyment." This, the IRS has ruled, means that the spouse really controls the trust fund, so it's included in her estate. In 1991, the Tax Court agreed with the IRS on this—the use of the word "comfort" in the trust documents cost the estate of Norman Vissering over $700,000! So be sure to read any trust documents carefully.

REST IN PEACE

A variation on the preceding strategy has become popular in estate planning. It's called a QTIP trust, and it's often used by married couples.

The ideal QTIP situation concerns second marriages. Lou Norris and Paula Stevens are both divorced, with children. When they marry each other, Paula has a considerably larger estate than Lou. Altogether, she has $2 million in assets.

When she revises her will, she retains the provision that leaves $600,000 to her children, sheltered by the estate tax credit. The other $1.4 million she leaves to Lou, in a QTIP trust.

According to the QTIP rules, all of the income from the trust must go to Lou. No one else can get any of this income. Similarly, the trustee can distribute money to Lou, in case of emergency, but to no one else. If all of these rules are followed, the QTIP trust is considered a spousal bequest, so there's no estate tax due.

At Lou's death, the trust assets will pass to Paula's children and estate tax will be due.

So what's the advantage of a QTIP? The estate tax can be deferred, if Lou dies after Paula. For all of Lou's life, he'll be able to live comfortably. Yet Paula can rest assured that her assets will ultimately wind up with her children, not with Lou's children. (If she had left all of her assets outright to Lou, estate tax would be deferred but he could have left those assets to his children.)

Any time one spouse has over $600,000 in assets, a QTIP should be considered. Take Carl Russell, a 40-year-old who owns a growing computer software company. He's happily married to Yvonne, the mother of his children.

But what would happen if Carl dies next month or next year or 10 years from now? Without a QTIP, Yvonne would inherit what might be a sizable amount, assuming Carl's company prospers. Then, Yvonne (who'd be a wealthy as well as an attractive widow) might remarry. Her new husband might have children of his own or they might have children together. Carl's money might wind up sending a bunch of strangers to Harvard, at the expense of his own children.

Instead, Carl sets up a QTIP. At his death, his estate gets the same tax deferral as it would if Carl had left the money outright to Yvonne. Not only will Yvonne have access to that money for her lifetime, she'll have a trustee to protect her from all the scavengers who prey on widows. And Carl knows his money will stay with his children, no matter what Yvonne does.

There are many technicalities to observe when you set up a QTIP: Not every attorney is familiar with the rules. So be sure you work with an experienced estate-planning lawyer if you create a QTIP.

SUMMING UP

- At your death, your executor must add up all of your assets and determine your net worth, for tax purposes.
- Under current law, all assets over $600,000 are subject to estate tax, with rates of 37 percent to 55 percent.
- The $600,000 threshold may be reduced, exposing more people to estate tax.
- Assets left to your spouse escape estate tax but the bill eventually will come due.
- To reduce estate tax, leave up to $600,000 to someone besides your spouse so you can use the tax exemption.
- If necessary, this bequest can be made in trust, providing lifetime security for your surviving spouse.
- With a QTIP trust, you provide a lifetime income to your spouse, yet you direct where those assets ultimately will wind up.

23 The Joy of Giving
Beat the Gift Tax as Well as the Estate Tax

Even if you shelter up to $1.2 million, as described in the previous chapter, your estate may still be exposed to tax. That's especially true if you're a business owner, a successful professional or executive, or if you inherited a sizable amount of money.

You might think you can shelter excess assets by giving them away. On her deathbed, Lilly May Watson, founder of a cosmetics empire, passes her fortune to her daughter, Betty Jean. Now Lilly May dies with scant assets so there's no estate tax.

That won't work. As mentioned, the gift tax is "unified" with the estate tax. Amounts that you give away are brought back into your estate, for tax purposes. If Lilly May gave away assets worth $3 million and dies with a net worth of $100,000, her estate would be taxed as if it were worth $3.1 million.

Nevertheless, there are ways to reduce your estate by making gifts. Under current law, everyone can give away up to $10,000 worth of assets each year, to any number of recipients. Married couples can give up to $20,000 a year.

Suppose Ken and Bonnie Jordan are retired, with total assets over $2 million. They have more than enough money to maintain their lifestyle and they want to reduce their estate tax liability.

They have two sons, both in solid marriages, and four grand-children. If they want, they can give up to $20,000 in assets to their two sons, two daughters-in-law, and four grandchildren. They can thus give away up to $160,000 a year (eight times $20,000), reducing their estates, and incur no gift tax consequences.

In addition to these $10,000 or $20,000 gifts, you can pay school tuition or medical bills for someone else, with no limit, without owing gift taxes. So Ken and Bonnie might pay their grandchildren's college bills, further shrinking their estates, as long as those payments are made directly to the schools.

The ability to make unlimited $10,000 or $20,000 annual gifts is a shelter that may be a prime target for tax "reformers." There might be an annual cap on such gifts. However, as long as that tax break is in place, anyone with estate tax concerns should take full advantage.

STRETCHING TWO TO MAKE SEVEN

You may even be able to top the $10,000/$20,000 limit, thanks to the Tax Court's 1991 decision in the Cristofani case. Maria Cristofani was a widow with two children. In 1984, she set up a trust, stating that the children, as primary beneficiaries, would inherit the trust prin-cipal at her death. At that time, her twin children were 35 years old, in good health.

Maria also named her five grandchildren as secondary benefi-ciaries. In case either of her children did not survive her by 120 days, that child's children would split half the trust.

After setting up the trust, Maria donated $70,000 worth of real estate to the trust in 1984 and in 1985. She filed no gift tax returns, taking the position that these were seven $10,000 gifts, to seven different recipients.

The IRS challenged this approach. According to the IRS, Maria was entitled to two $10,000 exclusions each year, for her children. The other $50,000 in annual gifts to the trust, though, were not excludable gifts to the five grandchildren, because there was little chance they'd get any of the trust assets.

But the Tax Court ruled for Cristofani. Each trust beneficiary, including the grandchildren, had the right to withdraw up to $10,000 worth of trust assets within 15 days after the gift was made. Thus, the grandchildren had a "present interest" in the gifts, which were allowed.

Based on the results of this case, you can make large gifts to a trust with secondary beneficiaries and owe no gift tax. This might help you slim down your estate in a short time period yet still keep the assets in the hands of a few chosen beneficiaries.

Although the Tax Court was unanimous on this issue, the IRS has indicated it will continue to fight in such circumstances. The IRS may even convince Congress to pass a law outlawing the practice. However, a trust created before any change in the law likely will stand up.

GIVEAWAY GAMES

If you decide to make gifts to reduce your estate, what should you give away? Don't give away assets, such as stocks or bonds, on which you have a paper loss. Instead, sell the assets yourself, claim the tax loss, and then give away the cash.

On the other hand, don't rush to give away appreciated assets. Sid Grant, for example, owns 500 shares of ABC Mutual Fund, which he bought at $12 apiece, currently priced at $20. He gives those shares to his daughter Jan. Because they're currently worth $10,000 (500 shares at $20), no gift tax is incurred.

However, Jan retains Sid's cost basis for the shares—$6,000. If she sells right away and receives $10,000, she'll have a $4,000 taxable gain.

Under current law, it's better for Sid to hold onto those shares until his death. Then, Jan can inherit with a stepped-up cost basis, equal to the value at Sid's death. The capital gain disappears.

There has been some talk about taxing capital gains at death, but the technical problems are substantial. If the rules are changed, it may make sense to give away appreciated assets, but the best strategy for now is:

1. Give away cash.
2. If cash is not available, give away assets with little or no capital gain or loss.

3. Give away appreciated assets if you have no other assets to give away. Your family is better off paying a 28 percent capital gains tax instead of a 50 percent estate tax.

APPRECIATION ANTICIPATION

You don't have to restrict your gifts to $10,000 or $20,000 a year. In some circumstances, it makes sense to make larger gifts while you're alive, effectively using up your estate tax exemption in advance.

For example, Barry Hillman owns a garden-supply company valued at $2 million. He gives away 45 percent of the company, valued at $900,000, to his two daughters. By doing so, he uses up his entire $600,000 estate tax exemption and incurs a taxable $300,000 taxable gift.

Why would he do this? Because he has removed 45 percent of his company from his estate. Future growth of his company will be 45 percent free of estate tax.

Suppose his company continues to grow, reaching $4 million in value at the time of his death. Assuming no further gifts, only $2.2 million worth of his company (the 55 percent he retained) will be included in his taxable estate. By making a $900,000 gift, Barry has sheltered $1.8 million worth of assets from tax.

If you're going to give away large chunks of assets, consider items likely to appreciate significantly. Shares in a family business are an example; another is real estate depressed by market conditions.

HOUSE GIFTS

Among the assets you may want to give away is your personal residence or a vacation home. If your estate will be subject to tax, giving away a $200,000 home can save around $100,000, plus future appreciation.

If you give away the house, it has to be a real gift. Change the homeowners insurance policy and the property tax registration to the name of the new owner. If you're going to continue living there—or using a vacation home—you should pay a fair-market rent. Otherwise, the IRS may contend the house really was part of your taxable estate.

One shelter you can use for such gifts is a "qualified personal residence trust." You give your house to the trust for a finite time period; during that period, you retain control of the house. When the trust expires, the house passes out of your estate to the beneficiaries, possibly your children.

As of this writing, real estate values are depressed in many parts of the United States. You can give a personal residence or a vacation home to a trust and legitimately use a low valuation, reducing gift tax. Yet you still have, say, 10 years' use of the property.

After the trust expires, you might want to retire and move somewhere else, letting your children take over the house. If you want to keep using it, you can pay rent to your children, the new owners.

Where's the shelter? A gift 10 years in the future is less valuable than a gift right now. Putting a $200,000 house in a 10-year trust, for example, reduces the value of the gift from $200,000 to less than $100,000. If you die before the trust expires, the house reverts to you and your estate is no worse off than when you started.

For example, Fran Foster, a 65-year-old widow, has a total estate of $1 million, including a house that was bought for $250,000 and is now valued at $500,000. If she dies with these holdings, her estate would owe about $150,000 in federal estate tax.

She sets up a trust with a 10-year term and transfers the house to it, retaining the right to live there. At the end of the term, the house will pass to her children. According to the IRS tables, such a future gift incurs a $150,000 gift tax.

Suppose Fran lives in the house for 10 years, then moves to Florida while her children take title to the house. Then Fran dies. Her assets, minus the house, are valued at $500,000. Adding her $150,000 taxable gift (the house), her total taxable estate is $650,000. So $50,000 worth of her assets are exposed to tax and her children owe $18,500 in federal estate tax.

If she had retained the house and it had grown to, say, $700,000 in value, she'd have had a $1.2 million estate and owed about

$235,000 in estate tax. So using the trust would save her family well over $200,000 in estate tax.

No Qualified Personal Residence Trust

Fran dies with a house worth	$ 700,000
Her other assets are worth	$ 500,000
Total estate	$1,200,000
Estate tax due	$ 235,000

Using Qualified Personal Residence Trust

Taxable gift of house is valued at	$ 150,000
Other assets are worth	$ 500,000
Unified gift and estate value	$ 650,000
Estate tax due	$ 18,500

Suppose the children sell the house then, for $700,000. With a $250,000 cost, they'd have a $450,000 gain. At 28 percent, they'd pay $126,000 in tax, a tax that could have been avoided if they had inherited the house outright. Altogether, then, using the trust saves Fran's family about $90,000 in tax.

There's another shelter that Fran might be able to use. Suppose, just before the trust term ends, she manages to raise $700,000 and buys the house back from the trust. When the trust terminates, the children get the $700,000 in cash, tax-free.

Fran, who now owns the house again, holds on until her death. Her children inherit the house with a step-up in basis, so they escape capital gains tax. Assuming Fran had to liquidate assets and borrow money to repurchase the house, her estate is not any larger and the estate tax is still minimal. Net tax saving from all this maneuvering: over $200,000.

Where are the drawbacks? Fran has to live in the house for 10 years. If she moves out, some of the tax benefit will be lost. (That's why vacation homes are especially suitable for this shelter.) After the trust term, if she wants to keep living there, she'll have to pay fair-market rent. If she dies before the trust term, the entire trans-action is annulled. As long as these obstacles don't seem insurmountable, using a personal-residence trust can be a six-figure tax shelter.

GIFTS FROM LIVING TRUSTS MAY BE DEADLY

Two basic estate-planning tools may not mix well. If you have a revocable living trust and plan to reduce estate taxes via lifetime gifts, you must be super careful to avoid saddling your heirs with killer taxes.

Trusts may be revocable or irrevocable. A revocable trust (that is, one that can be revoked) can be established only while you're alive. Typically, a revocable trust is under the complete control of the grantor (you) while the grantor lives. The purpose of shifting assets to this type of trust is to allow them to pass to your heirs without going through probate.

Revocable trusts help you avoid probate but they can't help you cut estate taxes. For tax reduction, you can give away assets while you're still alive, whether or not you have a revocable trust. Those assets, once they're outside of your possession, aren't included in your taxable estate.

However, under the Internal Revenue Code, gifts you make from revocable trusts within three years of your death are thrown back into your taxable estate and subjected to estate tax.

Suppose you transfer virtually all of your assets into a revocable trust to avoid probate. But you also want to give away assets and reduce estate tax. How can you make gifts and avoid the three-year rule? The IRS and the Tax Court have spelled out the do's and don'ts of making gifts from revocable trusts.

In 1991, the Tax Court heard the Estate of Jalkut case. Here, a revocable trust's trustee could make distributions only to the grantor, as long as the grantor was competent. However, after the grantor was no longer capable of managing his own affairs, the trustee could make distributions to others.

Gifts were made from the trust within three years of Jalkut's death, before and after his incompetency. The IRS assessed estate tax on all the assets given away in this three-year period.

The Tax Court ruled that all gifts made while the grantor was still competent were two-step transactions, trust-to-grantor-to-recipient. Thus, they were not subject to estate tax.

However, gifts made from the trust after the grantor's incompetency, within three years of death, were thrown back into the taxable estate. This decision conforms with IRS rulings.

So, if you're one of the many Americans who has set up a revocable trust, to avoid probate, you can avoid estate tax problems if you draw up a revocable trust that restricts the trustee to making distributions to you, the grantor. This will make all gifts two-step gifts, under the Jalkut ruling, but this limits flexibility.

The best strategy probably is to actually go through a two-step process when making gifts of assets held in a revocable trust. First, formally remove the assets from the trust and take title in your own name. Then, give away the assets. This will avoid the application of the three-year rule. Even some sophisticated estate-planning attorneys aren't aware of this pitfall, so don't assume your lawyer is up to speed.

LAST LAUGH

A final audit-proof tax shelter is to "vote with your feet." Move from a state with high estate tax to one that imposes little or none. Massachusetts is notorious for its high estate surtax—a $2 million estate will owe nearly $150,000 to the state, in addition to the federal levy. Other states with stiff death duties include Connecticut, Kentucky, Michigan, Iowa, South Dakota, North Carolina, New York, and Indiana.

Relief lies to the South and the West. Starting with South Carolina, you can move south to Florida, west to California, then north to Alaska, and pay little or no extra estate tax. The key, though, is to truly establish domicile in the low-tax state, as explained in Chapter 21.

SUMMING UP

- As long as you have enough assets to live out your life in comfort, plan on making gifts to reduce your taxable estate.
- You can give up to $10,000 per recipient per year without gift tax consequences. Married couples can give $20,000.
- In addition, you can pay someone else's medical or school bills.
- Thanks to a Tax Court ruling, you may be able to give away large chunks of assets to a trust with primary and secondary beneficiaries.
- When you make gifts, give away cash or unappreciated assets before giving away appreciated assets.
- If you hold assets likely to appreciate sharply, you may want to give them away even if they top the $10,000 or $20,000 limit.
- Using a qualified personal residence trust may be a way to save large sums while passing a home or vacation house to your kids.
- Many people create revocable trusts, while they're alive, to avoid probate. If you make gifts from a revocable trust, the assets may be included in your taxable estate.
- To avoid this problem, remove assets from a revocable trust, change the title to your own name, and then make gifts.
- Moving to the South or the West may save large amounts of state estate tax, as long as you make sure your move is well documented.

Glossary

Accommodator. Third party brought into a like-kind exchange (see definition). The accommodator holds one of the properties or sales proceeds until a three-way deferred exchange can be completed.

Actuary. A mathematician who calculates probable future rates of return to determine the amount of annual contributions to a defined-benefit plan.

Adjusted gross income (AGI). On a tax return, gross income minus various deductions (e.g., retirement plan contributions, moving expenses, alimony payments). For many tax deductions, eligibility is determined by the level of AGI.

Adjusted sales price. Selling price of a personal residence, minus selling costs and fix-up expenses incurred within 90 days of the sale.

Alternative minimum tax (AMT). An income tax that's calculated after various deductions and preferences are added back to taxable income. Taxpayers pay the AMT if the obligation is greater than the regular income tax obligation.

Annuity. A series of fixed payments at regular intervals, usually monthly.

Annuity trust. A form of charitable remainder trust in which the annual payout to the income beneficiaries is fixed.

Appreciated securities. Stocks or bonds that have gone up in value. Giving such securities to charity avoids paying tax on the capital gain so it's usually preferable to paying cash.

Assessor. Local official who determines the value of real estate for the purpose of setting property tax.

Bailout clause. A provision in a fixed annuity. If the rate of return is renewed below a preset number, investors can switch to another annuity without paying a surrender charge.

Basis. Cost of an asset for tax purposes. The basis of a security is generally the price paid for it. The basis of a principal residence is the purchase price plus the cost of capital improvements. The basis of investment property is the purchase price minus accumulated depreciation.

Bond call. The issuer's right to redeem outstanding bonds before their scheduled maturity. Calls usually are exercised when interest rates have fallen, permitting the issuer to reduce interest payments. Therefore, investors have to reinvest at lower rates.

Boot. Cash or other consideration paid to even up the values in a like-kind exchange. Typically, boot is taxable.

Capital improvement. Money spent on real estate, including a personal residence, that adds long-lasting value to the property.

Cash equivalent. A savings vehicle with virtually no transaction costs or risk of principal loss, where you have easy access to your money. Examples include bank accounts, money market funds, and Treasury bills.

Cash value. Investment account inside a permanent life insurance policy. Money accumulates inside an insurance policy, free of current taxes. If necessary, policyholders can access their cash value through loans or withdrawals.

Certificate of participation (COP). A municipal bond issued to purchase equipment or property on an installment basis. Funding to cover a COP's interest and principal repayment must be approved each year in the issuer's budget.

Charitable remainder trust. A trust that pays income to individuals while they're alive, then distributes the remainder of its assets to charity. Creating a charitable remainder trust is an excellent way to convert appreciated but low-income property to income-producing securities without paying a large tax bill.

Closed-end fund. A fund with a limited number of shares outstanding. The shares trade like common stocks, on an exchange. Closed-end funds may hold stocks or bonds. They're actively managed, meaning that the manager can sell holdings and buy new ones.

Corporation. A legal entity chartered by a state or by the federal government. The advantages of incorporation include limited liability for shareholders, liquidity of corporate stock, and continuity of existence. However, corporations may have to pay corporate income tax, in addition to personal income tax owed on employees' compensation and owners' dividends.

Credit-shelter trust. A trust designed to take advantage of the tax credit to which all estates are entitled. Typically, an amount equal to the maximum that can be sheltered is left in trust to the next generation, with the surviving spouse entitled to lifetime income. Also called a "bypass trust."

Crummey power. The right of a trustee to withdraw money from a trust during a certain time period. This right—even if it's not exercised—gives a trust beneficiary a "present interest" in gifts to the trust, which can lead to an exclusion from gift tax.

Custodian. An individual or institution that keeps custody of assets, often for a minor or a retirement plan participant.

Decline curve. Measure of production from an oil and gas well. Typically, production is highest in the first year, tapering off in the future.

Deduction equivalent. A tax credit that provides the tax savings equal to a certain amount of tax deductions. For example, in a 28%

tax bracket, a $25,000 deduction reduces taxes by $7,000. In this situation, a $7,000 tax credit is a $25,000 deduction equivalent.

Deferred annuity. An annuity contract in which a payment or payments are made prior to the beginning of the income stream. The money paid for the annuity compounds, free of current taxes, until the contract is annuitized (converted to an annuity).

Defined-benefit plan. A pension plan that promises to pay a specific amount to all participants after they retire, provided they have been in the plan for a certain number of years. Payouts are determined by the participant's compensation and years of service covered by the plan. In these plans, the employer bears the risk, promising a certain level of retirement income.

Defined-contribution plan. Qualified retirement plan in which employers or the self-employed contribute each year. Contributions are credited to a separate account for each participant. Retirement income from such plans is not guaranteed, but depends upon investment performance during the interim period. Therefore, the employee, not the employer, bears the risk of higher or lower retirement income.

Depletion allowance. Tax deduction available to companies that extract oil, gas, coal, and other minerals. Oil and gas limited partnerships can pass the deduction through to their limited partners.

Depreciation. A tax deduction that reflects the loss of value of an asset due to wear and tear or obsolescence.

Developmental drilling. Exploration for oil and gas in an area where oil and gas previously have been discovered. There is a high probability of discovering oil and gas. However, such wells tend to produce modest or even skimpy amounts of oil and gas.

Dividend. A distribution of corporate profits to shareholders. Owners of private businesses often try to avoid paying dividends because they're not tax-deductible for the corporation, yet they are taxable for the recipients.

Domicile. The place of a person's principal residence, for legal purposes, including state taxes.

Easement. An interest in real property held by a party besides the owner. Easements often are granted by deed. Investors in historical rehabilitation projects may donate an easement to a local preservation society, promising that the building's facade will not be altered. The value of this donation may be taken as a charitable deduction.

Executor. Person or institution responsible for seeing that the provisions of a will are carried out. If a person dies without a will, a court will appoint an executor to handle property transfers. Also called a "personal representative."

Fiduciary. A person who holds assets in trust for a beneficiary. A fiduciary is responsible for investing trust assets prudently.

Fixed annuity. A deferred annuity in which a certain return is set for a certain time period. At the end of that time period, the return is reset. Fixed annuities generally pay about the same as high-quality bonds.

Flexible spending accounts (FSAs). An employee benefit in which employees pay for various costs with money deducted from their paychecks before taxes. The amount is preselected each year by the employee, up to certain limits, and channeled into specific accounts (e.g., unreimbursed medical expenses, dependent-care costs). Purchases are then made from these accounts.

Flush production. An early spurt of production from an oil and gas well, which typically declines in succeeding years.

Forward averaging. Calculating a tax obligation as if the amount involved was earned over a period of years, which reduces tax rates. Five- and 10-year averaging may be available for lump-sum retirement distributions. The tax is due in one year, however.

401(k) plan. A retirement plan in which employees elect to reduce their salary and contribute the money into an investment pool. Contributions and earnings compound, tax-deferred, until the employee retires or leaves the company.

General obligation bond. A municipal bond backed by all the taxing power of the issuer.

General partner. All partners in a regular partnership are general partners, responsible for the partnership's liabilities. In a limited partnership, the general partner manages the business operation. Before investing in a limited partnership, it is crucial to check on the skill and experience of the general partner.

Ginnie Mae. A mortgage-backed security guaranteed by the Government National Mortgage Association (GNMA). Investors collect mortgage principal and interest payments from a pool of homeowners. Ginnie Maes are backed by the full faith and credit of the federal government. Yields tend to be a bit higher than rates on Treasury bonds but the income stream is uncertain because prepayments are erratic.

Grantor. The creator of a trust, usually the person who transfers assets into it. Also called the "maker," the "settlor," and the "trustor."

Guaranteed investment contract (GIC). A contract between an insurance company and a retirement plan in which the insurer guarantees a specific rate of return for a specific time period. The "guarantee" is only from the insurance company, not from any government agency.

Historic rehab tax credit. A tax credit for fixing up a building deemed historic by a preservation society, or a building in a historic district. If all the criteria are met, the credit is 20% of the rehabilitation costs.

Home equity. The current market value of a house, minus outstanding debt secured by that house.

Home equity loan. A line of credit secured by a principal residence or by a second home. Borrowers tap the line for money as needed and pay interest on the amount that's outstanding. The interest is tax-deductible, in most cases.

Immediate annuity. An annuity where the payment stream begins right away. Each payment is part taxable, part a tax-free return of the money paid to buy the annuity.

Independent contractor. A worker who's not an employee. The IRS has a list of 20 points it uses to differentiate. In general, independent contractors have multiple sources of income and control the manner in which they work.

Individual Retirement Account (IRA). A personal retirement program for employed individuals. Deposits (up to $2,000 per year) must be made into an account with proper certification. The amount of the deposit that's deductible depends on the individual's income and coverage by other plans.

In-state fund. A municipal bond fund holding issues from a single state. For investors who live in that state, interest is generally exempt from state income tax and perhaps from local income tax as well.

Intangible drilling costs. The costs incurred in drilling and completing oil and gas wells. Such costs are currently deductible, thanks to a special tax break. In other lines of business, similar costs must be deducted over a period of several years.

Irrevocable trust. A trust that can't be revoked or materially altered after it has been created.

Joint-and-survivor annuity. An annuity that pays two or more recipients, often a husband and wife. After one recipient dies, the survivor continues to receive payments. Joint-and-survivor annuities may have the lowest payout rate among annuities.

Joint-and-survivor pension. A pension that pays two or more recipients, as long as either survives. In some cases, the survivor's pension is reduced.

Joint venture. A specific project financed and supported by two or more parties.

Jointly owned property. Property owned by two or more people. When one dies, the other(s) takes over ownership, no matter what is stated in a will. Such property does not pass through probate, but it may be subject to estate tax. Also known as "joint tenancy with right of survivorship."

Keogh plan. A retirement plan in which a self-employed person can make tax-deductible contributions. In the plan documents, the proprietor spells out whether the plan will be a defined-benefit plan or a defined-contribution plan.

Kiddie tax. Tax treatment of dependents under age 14. In excess of certain limits, unearned income is taxed as if it were earned by the parents.

Leveraged closed-end fund. A closed-end fund that borrows money, usually by borrowing short-term at low rates. The money is then invested in longer-term, higher-yield assets, driving up the fund's overall yield. Such funds are vulnerable to rising short-term interest rates.

Lien. A creditor's claim against property. When a taxpayer moves from one state to another, and the old state assesses tax, a lien may be placed on property left in the old state, if the tax isn't paid. In some cases, property may be seized to satisfy the lien.

Like-kind exchange. A swap of one kind of investment property for another. If values are equal, capital gains tax can be deferred. Also called a tax-deferred exchange or a tax-free exchange.

Limited partnership. A business structure consisting of limited partners and general partners. Limited partners typically invest money but they are not responsible for partnership debts or liabilities. They can't participate in management decisions. All decisions are made by the general partner or partners, who are responsible for partnership liabilities.

Liquidating distribution. The sale proceeds after a corporation has been sold.

Liquidity. The ability to convert an asset to cash quickly, without paying sizable transaction fees.

Living trust. A trust set up while the creator is alive (as opposed to a testamentary trust, created at death).

Long-term capital gain. The gain on the sale of an asset held more than one year. Long-term capital gains may be taxed less than other forms of income.

Low-income housing tax credit. A tax credit available to investors who buy or rehabilitate housing, then rent to qualified tenants. This credit is available for 10 straight years, as long as the property remains rented to low-income tenants.

Lump-sum distribution. A single payment to the beneficiary of a retirement plan, covering the entire amount in that beneficiary's account.

Marginal tax rate. The tax owed on your last dollar of income. If, for example, going from a $30,000 income to a $31,000 income increases your tax bill by $280, the marginal tax rate is 28%. Also known as your tax bracket.

Master limited partnership (MLP). A limited partnership trading like a common stock. MLPs are not subject to the corporate income tax. Often, MLPs pay high dividends, partially tax-sheltered, because deductions can be passed through to investors. MLPs are also known as publicly traded partnerships.

Modified endowment contract (MEC). A life insurance policy that's bought with a single premium payment, or a few payments. Unlike regular insurance policies, loans or withdrawals from MECs are probably taxable and subject to a 10% penalty tax before age 59-1/2.

Money-purchase plan. A form of defined-contribution plan in which the employer is required to make a certain level of contribution each year, regardless of the employer's financial results.

Municipal bond. Bonds issued by state or local governments and their agencies. Interest on these bonds is exempt from federal income tax. In some cases, locally issued municipal bonds are also exempt from state and local income tax.

Net asset value (NAV). The market value of a mutual fund share. NAV is calculated by taking the value of all securities held by the fund, then adding cash and other assets. From total assets, total liabilities are subtracted. The result is then divided by the number of shares outstanding.

Net capital loss. The excess of capital losses over capital gains. Net capital losses can be deducted up to $3,000 per year. Larger losses must be carried forward to future years.

Net operating income (NOI). The profit from a venture after subtracting operating expenses, insurance, and taxes but before subtracting interest expense.

Nonrecourse debt. A loan not backed by the borrower's personal assets. In case of default, the lender may seize only the collateral securing the loan. On the other hand, recourse debt is backed by all of a borrower's assets, which can be seized in case of default.

Open-end fund. A traditional mutual fund. They're "open-end" because they continually sell shares to new investors or redeem shares when investors want cash.

Partnership. An agreement between two or more parties to operate a business, sharing in the work and expense as well as in the profits. Partnerships owe no income tax. Instead, each partner pays tax on his or her share of partnership income. Partnerships may be general partnerships or limited partnerships (see definitions).

Passive income. Taxable income from an investment in which you don't actively participate. Losses from such activities are passive losses. Passive losses cannot be used to offset income from other sources, with few exceptions.

Pension. Retirement income from a former employer.

Percentage depletion. An advantageous form of the depletion allowance. An investor in a successful drilling fund may be able to write off more than the original investment, over a period of years, via percentage depletion.

Permanent life insurance. Life insurance that stays in force for the policyholder's lifetime, unless the policy is canceled or lapses. Premiums usually are fixed, year after year. An investment account called the "cash value" may be tapped via loans or withdrawals.

Personal residence trust. A trust used to transfer a house from one generation to the next. Typically, the older generation transfers the house to the trust and retains the right to live there during the trust term. Then the house passes to the beneficiaries. Because the gift is a future gift, the house gets a much lower value for gift tax purposes.

Prerefunded bond. A municipal bond that is backed by Treasury bonds, so they're extremely safe. Most prerefunded bonds are called within a few years.

Present interest. The right to enjoy assets immediately. As long as the recipients have a present interest in a gift, donors can give up to $10,000 per year per recipient without incurring gift tax. Married couples can give up to $20,000.

Present value. The value today of a future payment or stream of payments. Assumptions must be made about return on investment in the interim.

Primary beneficiaries. Trust beneficiaries with the first call on trust income and assets.

Prime rate. The interest rate for short-term loans that banks charge to their most creditworthy customers.

Private placement. An investment sold directly to a limited number of investors, typically institutions or wealthy individuals.

Private purpose municipal bonds. Bonds issued to finance certain ventures such as housing projects or student loans. Like all municipal bonds, interest is exempt from regular income tax, but the interest may be subject to the alternative minimum tax (AMT) for investors with substantial deductions or preference items.

Probate. The process of "proving" a will, or handling the estate of a person who dies without a will. Under court supervision, the title of the decedent's assets is transferred to new owners.

Profit-sharing plan. A retirement plan in which an employer makes contributions, at its discretion, to an account for each employee. Employers have a great deal of flexibility on contributions.

Qualified retirement plan. A plan set up by an employer for employees that qualifies for benefits under the tax code. The employer makes the payments to the plan and is entitled to deductions. The employees pay tax only when they withdraw money.

Qualified terminable interest property (QTIP) trust. Such a trust is left by one spouse to another. The survivor is entitled to all the income and access to the principal in an emergency; no one else can have any access to the trust. Thus, assets transferred to a QTIP escape gift and estate tax. However, the creator of the trust is the one who determines where the assets will go after the survivor dies.

Real estate investment trust (REIT). A company that holds a portfolio of real estate investments. Equity REITs own properties, while mortgage REITs make mortgage loans. Most REITs are publicly traded. In order to avoid the corporate income tax, nearly all of a REIT's income must be distributed to investors.

Rehabilitation tax credit. A tax credit earned for fixing up buildings placed in service before 1936. If all the criteria are met, the credit is 10% of the rehabilitation cost.

Revocable trust. A trust that can be revoked. Such trusts usually have no tax advantages but trust assets avoid probate.

Revenue bond. A municipal bond issued to finance a specific project such as a toll bridge or a hospital. Revenue bonds are paid off with funds generated by that project.

Reverse split-dollar life insurance. A variation of split-dollar life insurance (see definition) in which a corporation provides for the retirement of the owner, and perhaps other key employees, without extending that coverage to all employees.

Rollover. The movement of funds from one vehicle to another. An IRA rollover is a transfer from a retirement plan to an IRA, with no tax obligation. Also, a loan renewal.

S corporation. A corporation that's taxed as a partnership, thus avoiding the corporate income tax. All corporate income is taxed to the shareholders personally, on a pro rata basis. Certain criteria must be met to qualify as an S corporation; if those criteria are met, S corporation status may be elected.

Secondary beneficiaries. Trust beneficiaries who will receive trust income and assets if the primary beneficiaries are unable to do so.

Secondary market. Market where securities are bought and sold after they've been issued.

Second mortgage. A mortgage secured by an asset, often a house, that is already mortgaged. In case of a default, the holder of a second mortgage will collect only after the holder of the first mortgage collects. Because the risk is greater, the interest on a second mortgage will be higher than the interest on a first mortgage.

Second-to-die life insurance. An insurance policy that pays off after two deaths. Because the insurance company's payment likely will be delayed, premiums are relatively low. Often, these policies cover a married couple, with the proceeds going to their children. Those proceeds can be used to pay estate tax. These policies also are called "survivorship" insurance policies.

Seven-pay test. The tax code requirement that insurance policies must meet in order for policy loans to be tax-free. In essence, the policy must be bought with a series of roughly equal payments.

Shared-equity financing arrangement (SEFA). An agreement in which one party helps another, often a grown child or an aging parent, to buy a home. For the best tax results, tax deductions (including depreciation) should be weighted toward the party with the higher tax bracket.

Short sale against the box. A short sale is a sale of borrowed stock. If the stock goes down, the investor makes money. In a short sale against the box, the investor sells short appreciated stocks already owned. The object is to lock in a gain on a stock but defer realization of the gain until the following year.

Simplified employee plan (SEP). A retirement plan in which both employee and employer contribute to an IRA. Employees are vested immediately and pay no tax on the employer's contributions. Employee contributions are tax-deferred until withdrawn, as are all earnings within the SEP. Employers may anticipate social security income when calculating SEP contributions, which favors highly-paid participants.

Single-life annuity. An annuity that pays an income as long as the recipient lives. After the recipient dies, no further payments are due. Single-life annuities usually have the highest payout of any form of annuity.

Single-premium deferred annuity. A deferred annuity bought with one fairly large payment, often $25,000 or more.

Sole proprietorship. An unincorporated business entity that's not a partnership. Income is taxed directly to the sole proprietor.

Split annuity. An investment strategy in which half of the money is placed in an immediate annuity, for high current income, while the other half is placed in a deferred annuity, to retain principal.

Split-dollar life insurance. An arrangement in which payments for life insurance are split between two or more parties. Typically, those parties are a corporation and an employee, often an owner-executive. Thanks to the structure of the tax code, the employee may get substantial coverage at little personal cost.

Standard deduction. A deduction available to all taxpayers filing federal income tax returns. Taxpayers with substantial deductions for mortgage interest, state and local taxes, and other areas are better off itemizing deductions instead of taking the standard deduction.

Step-up in basis. Increase in basis (see definition) from the original basis to the current value. Under current law, basis is stepped up at the owner's death. Thus, the heirs can sell the property right away and owe no capital gains tax.

Surrender charge. Payment for premature withdrawal from a deferred annuity. Often, these charges are substantial (5%–10%) in the first year, slowly tapering down to nothing after five or 10 years.

Tax-bracket arbitrage. A strategy involving two parties in which tax deductions are shifted to the party with the higher bracket or income to the party with the lower bracket.

Tax credit. A direct reduction of your tax obligation. A $1,000 tax credit, for example, reduces a $10,000 tax obligation to $9,000. In contrast, a tax deduction reduces your taxable income, and the tax savings are determined by your marginal tax rate. In a 28% tax bracket, a $1,000 deduction reduces a tax obligation by $280.

Tax preference item. A tax break that taxpayers must take back into income when calculating liability for the alternative minimum tax. Examples include excess depletion deductions, intangible drilling costs, and interest on private activity municipal bonds.

Term-certain payout. An annuity payout option in which payments are guaranteed for at least a certain number of years. If the recipient dies before the end of the period, the remaining payments are made to beneficiaries. Term-certain payments often are lower than single-life annuities, higher than joint-and-survivor annuities. They're also called a "period-certain" annuity.

Term life insurance. Insurance that's written for a specific time period, for which the policyholder pays only for a death benefit. Premiums increase as the policyholder grows older. There is no cash value.

Trust. A fictional entity created to hold assets for a beneficiary or beneficiaries.

Trustee. An individual or institution who holds title to property held in trust. The trustee is responsible for managing the trust assets.

Unified federal gift and estate tax. At death, taxes based on wealth are called estate taxes. To prevent people from giving away their assets and thus avoiding estate tax, a federal gift tax is imposed, integrated with the estate tax.

Unit. Share in certain investments, such as unit investment trusts and limited partnerships.

Unit investment trust. An investment vehicle that purchases a fixed portfolio of securities, often municipal bonds. Investors buy units of the trust and receive a portion of the income. The portfolio of securities remains constant until the bonds mature.

Unitrust. A form of charitable remainder trust in which the annual payout to the income beneficiary varies. The payout is a percentage of trust assets, which varies from year to year.

Unlimited marital deduction. One spouse can give or bequeath an unlimited amount of assets to the other spouse. The gift or bequest is deductible from gift or estate tax, so no tax is due.

Variable annuity. A deferred annuity in which your account value will vary, over the years, depending upon investment performance. Investors usually can allocate their accounts among several investment choices, including stock funds and bond funds. Successful investors can build up large accounts while unsuccessful investors can lose money.

Variable life insurance. A form of permanent life insurance in which policyholders can direct their premiums to different investment vehicles, including stock funds and bond funds. The more successful the investment decisions, the greater the policy's cash value. Cash value may decline in case of poor investments.

Zero-coupon bond. A bond that pays no interest until maturity. Then, all the accrued interest, plus interest on that interest, is paid. Zero-coupon municipal bonds, which are tax-exempt, are used for certain special purposes such as deferring payouts from charitable remainder trusts.

Index